ESSENTIALS OF THE NEW SCIENCE OF LEARNING

This streamlined adaption of the best-selling book *The New Science of Learning: How to Learn in Harmony With Your Brain* is a distillation of the most essential and immediately effective tips and strategies selected specifically to put college students on the path to success.

In this primer, Zakrajsek masterfully translates complex findings from cognitive psychology and neuroscience into easy-to-understand concepts that can be used immediately to learn faster and retain information longer. Readers will come away with strategies that have been demonstrated throughout the world to improve learning, as well as a greatly enhanced understanding of how the learning process works. Taking just a few hours to read the material in this book and practice what has been assembled for learners at any level may well prove to be one of the best decisions a college student can make.

Essentials of the New Science of Learning: The Power of Learning in Harmony With Your Brain is ideal for individual student use or as a powerful supplement to any course, in any course, across the college curriculum.

Todd D. Zakrajsek is Research Associate Director in the School of Medicine at the University of North Carolina at Chapel Hill, USA. This is Dr. Zakrajsek's seventh book related to better teaching and enhanced student learning. He also directs four annual Lilly Conferences on Evidence-Based Teaching and Learning and has given workshops and keynote addresses in 49 US states and 12 countries.

ESSENTIALS OF THE NEW SCIENCE OF LEARNING

The Power of Learning in Harmony With Your Brain

Todd D. Zakrajsek

Taylor & Francis Group

NEW YORK AND LONDON

Designed cover image: Getty Images

First published 2025
by Routledge
605 Third Avenue, New York, NY 10158

and by Routledge
4 Park Square, Milton Park, Abingdon, Oxon, OX14 4RN

Routledge is an imprint of the Taylor & Francis Group, an informa business

ISBN: 978-1-032-81304-2 (hbk)
ISBN: 978-1-032-80475-0 (pbk)
ISBN: 978-1-003-49917-6 (ebk)

DOI: 10.4324/9781003499176

Typeset in Times New Roman
by codeMantra

This book is dedicated to McKenzie Baker. There are too few truly remarkable people in this world. McKenzie is one, and even among that select group, she is a beacon. I will write for as long as her deft editorial light shines the way.

CONTENTS

ACKNOWLEDGMENTS

Regardless of the name on the cover, books are never the product of one or even a few people. This book is no exception. My family has provided extensive assistance on this project. Debra pored over multiple drafts, listened to me think out loud about what I was about to write, and helped me to shape the overall structure of the manuscript. My daughters, Emma, MaryHelen, and Kathryn, and my sons-in-law, Ryan and Liam, each with varied college experience, provided insights into the life of students and added depth to concepts throughout the book. Watching my grandchildren, Matthew, Preston, Lorelei, Theo, and Ollie grow continues to inspire me with the speed at which learning transpires. Sincere appreciation goes out to John Gardner for his authority and expertise in shaping much of what the first-year experience and undergraduate education are today. John von Knorring was instrumental in helping the foundation of this project come into reality. He has been a friend and mentor, providing expert feedback for several of my projects, some published and others not. My new friend at Routledge, Alex Andrews, emerged on the scene just as I was about to stop writing altogether and provided inspiration for me to get back to the keyboard. There are countless others, of course, too many to mention here, who have helped me become the educator I am today, such as friends in the world of faculty development, campus colleagues from every discipline imaginable, and psychologists from across the country. Finally, I recognize and thank the learners who have tolerated me as I worked diligently at becoming an increasingly effective teacher, knowing full well that I will never be as good as they deserve. Literally thousands of individuals, each contributing in their own way, made it possible for me to accumulate and then share my experience in hopes that this book will help students find a way to become stronger learners by learning how to learn. To all those noted above, you have my deepest appreciation.

INTRODUCTION

Welcome to *Essentials of the New Science of Learning: The Power of Learning in Harmony With Your Brain.* When the first edition of *The New Science of Learning* was written in 2013, it was designed as an ancillary resource to classes so students could learn about learning while learning the content in the course. Due to the popularity of the first edition, a second was written, and then a third edition in 2022. The problem is that teachers are good at addition and terrible at subtraction. As a result, each edition of this book ended up containing significantly more information. The longer books work well for additional information about learning, but are not ideally suited to be an ancillary resource. As a result, this brief guide was written as a more streamlined version of the third edition and about the length of the first edition. Mostly, what was cut to create this version relates to deeper dives into the context and background of the strategies presented. Some of the cuts allowed for new material and examples not found in the third edition of *The New Science of Learning*, particularly in the area of generative artificial intelligence. *The New Science of Learning: How to Learn in Harmony With Your Brain* has been one of the best-selling books in higher education devoted to helping students be better, stronger learners. I hope you find this brief version just as helpful. Overall, my goal remains to bring together information from many sources and present it to you in a succinct manner to give you research-informed strategies for learning that you can apply in any course and after graduation.

Your Host

This book is influenced extensively by my life as a student, a learner, a faculty member, and a parent. I have shared a bit about myself in several of the chapters so you get a better sense of my perspectives on and versions of the material selected and presented. You will also see that individuals who are college professors and book authors also struggle with learning at times. I think there is value in you knowing a bit about me as you read this book. I also hope you'll see how other books you read are influenced by those who write the books, even though authors rarely reveal themselves to their readers.

As you read this book, I, Dr. Todd Zakrajsek, will be your host for this learning adventure. College was often challenging for me. I was the first person in my family to go to college. I still remember the excitement that fall as my parents drove me to a small college in northern Michigan. After settling into my dorm room, I was nervous but couldn't wait for classes to start. As classes began, I started thinking about what it would be like to earn a college degree in criminal justice and become a Michigan State Police officer.

It didn't go as planned. Just about a month into my new adventure, I nearly flunked out. I received an F minus minus (it turns out they have those) on a chemistry test, an F plus (yes, those as well) on a physics test, and a D minus on an Intro to Criminal Justice test. I recall thinking that none of this made any sense. High school had been easy—I cruised along with high Bs and low As with next to no studying. Failing a test was foreign to me; the idea of failing multiple tests was inconceivable. After doing so poorly on my first set of exams, I concluded that I was "high school smart," but not "college smart." Frustrated and embarrassed, I began the process of withdrawing from college. It was depressing.

After getting four of the five necessary faculty signatures to complete the withdrawal form, I needed only my Intro Psych professor, Dr. Sawyer, to add his name to the form, and college would be over for me. He asked why I decided to drop out, and then explained that it wasn't my intelligence that was the problem. He said I had to figure out the difference between being familiar with the content and knowing the content. His advice was simple but challenging: Find a different way to learn. I went to the library and found an old copy of *The Memory Book* (Lorayne & Lucas, 1975). At the time, I didn't know there were books written to help people remember and books about learning how to learn. The book helped. The following month was a bit better, and so was the next and the next after that. I read more books on learning, and about a year later I switched my major from criminal justice to psychology. My story continues at the end of this book in the section titled, A message from Dr. Z.

So, how did I go from nearly flunking out of college after just 1 month to graduating and then going on to earn a PhD in psychology? By learning how to learn in harmony with my brain, which is so important that it is the subtitle of this book. In this book, you will find strategies, tips, suggestions, and research about how best to learn. I have presented the information in this book to undergraduate and graduate students throughout the United States. Students regularly come up after the presentations and ask why nobody told them this information before. I understand their frustration. Nobody told me this information either, and it almost took me out of college before the end of my first term. Like many of you, I didn't know there were strategies to make a person a stronger learner. I find it odd that learning how to learn is not taught systematically throughout school. Without knowing more about how to learn, many students waste hundreds of hours of study time, and way too many good students flunk out of college, just like I nearly did. Many of the students who struggle in college don't lack the intelligence to succeed. They just don't know how to learn effectively. The good news is that you can change that *right now* and take better advantage of the learning opportunities college offers.

Where This Book Came From

So, where did I find the information on learning how to learn that is included in this book? It turns out there is a staggering amount of research about the science of learning, with new articles published every day. When teaching, I do my best to break the studies down so that my undergraduate students find the material interesting. To write this book, I pulled together much of the information I had that applied to learning how to learn. The work presented is designed to empower you as a lifelong learner to experience more classroom success and carry forward skills outside the classroom. The research in this book comes from a wide variety of areas: neuroscience, cognitive psychology, social psychology, motivation, and others. It is a lot, but don't worry, everything will be explained in a way that is easy to understand.

Throughout this book, you will find strategies that you can use to help you take exams, write papers, interact in class, and work in groups. Often relatively straightforward changes can have a significant impact on your learning. Although not all strategies work for all people, research on information processing, learning, and memory shows remarkable consistency across a wide variety of learners. By trying different strategies, you will find what works for you and what doesn't. You will find that everyone struggles with learning at times and that failure is often an important learning experience. The secret is to learn every time you fail and keep learning to learn even more.

We are all unique, but nearly all people share common learning functions when encountering similar learning situations. You don't get better just by doing something. You get better at something (e.g., taking tests, driving, baking) by working at getting better at some aspect of it (e.g., trying new study strategies, driving on different surfaces, experimenting with types of sugar). If you learn about and apply evidence-based strategies, like those in this book, to specific areas you wish to improve, you will get better at learning. Increasingly, you will be learning in harmony with your brain.

The Structure of This Brief Edition

The information in this book is carefully laid out for you. Each chapter describes different aspects pertaining to how learning works and ways to apply what you are learning. There are study tips and discussion questions in each chapter designed to help you think about the material, to reflect on how it may help you, and suggestions for putting it to use. The chapters can stand alone and can be read in any order.

Learning requires work, but I have done my best to make the information in this book interesting, accessible, and applicable. I hope you even find it fun at times. There are so many possibilities once you learn how to learn in harmony with your brain.

A Note to Students

This book addresses the many issues I have seen students struggle with in my time as a college faculty member. The demands of college are generally very different from what you've encountered before, and I hope that this material, together with your effort, will help you excel in your academic studies.

Now that you have the opportunity to pursue a college degree, you need to do the work to succeed. You can do this, but it won't be easy. Things of value rarely are. I am confident that the information you learn will help you succeed. My final piece of advice as we get started is to work through the challenges and celebrate your successes. I wish you well.

Note: I use the word "college" in place of "college and university" throughout this book, only to make it less clunky to read. The content is equally relevant whether you're at a college, technical school, or university.

Discussion Questions

1 What do you find easiest to learn? Why do you think that new information in the area you noted is so easy for you to learn? What about an area in which you struggle? What makes that area so challenging?
2 Find and read one article that contains something about how people learn. What was the major overall finding or point in the article about learning that would help you to be a stronger learner?

Reference

Lorayne, H., & Lucas, J. (1975). *The memory book: The classic guide to improving your memory at work, at school, and at play.* Random House.

PART 1
Set Up for Success

1

LEARNING FROM MULTIPLE PERSPECTIVES

Everyone has a perspective unlike anyone else's, based on circumstances faced, opportunities presented, and choices made. Some perspectives are influenced by how individuals are treated, often based on factors such as clothing choices, general physical condition, and skin color. These visual clues are, unfortunately, often used to make unfounded assumptions about how a person might react to a given issue. The challenge is that until we begin to interact with someone, we don't know much about their circumstances or their perspectives of the world around them. For example, an older individual who looks haggard and dirty approaching you on a street corner may give you the expectation that they are homeless and about to ask you for money. A younger person wearing a college sweatshirt approaching you on the same street corner may bring up an expectation that they are going to ask directions. The visual prejudging that occurs without interacting and listening to them creates biases. And such biases impede our ability to understand the perspectives of others. What is too frequently devalued, or missed altogether, is that which can't be seen, the lived experiences that make each person an individual.

Conversations in the college classroom allow us the opportunity to learn about the perspectives of others based on their actual lived experiences. It is rarely discussed, but *that* is one of the most valuable outcomes of a college education. Yes, what you learn in class is important, as is the degree you earn when you finish. But an important part of college is the opportunity to broaden your perspective by learning alongside individuals who hold very different perspectives than yours. You won't agree with everyone; however, if you listen to them and think about what they have to say, it will help you better understand yourself and your perspective even if you never agree.

DOI: 10.4324/9781003499176-2

In the classes you take, engaging with others who think differently than you brings a richness already mentioned, but it also bring challenges. The following concepts are just a few things to keep in mind as you encounter new, exciting, and challenging viewpoints. Learning in harmony with your brain starts with how you choose to interact with the world around you.

Dichotomous Thinking

I have long argued that *dichotomous thinking* is weak thinking. A *dichotomy* is something divided into two parts—black or white, up or down, day or night. The world is much easier to navigate using this simplistic view, so it is attractive to many. However, dichotomous thinking results in a resistance to consider details, to see the complexity of something, and in the process errors in judgment are made. Dichotomous thinkers often dig in on an issue and are resistant to potential alternative views.

The value of learning from multiple perspectives is that it allows a person to become a critical thinker, moving from shouting down anyone who disagrees with their specific position to better understanding that the position is likely more complicated than it appears on the surface. This is important because you can't solve major league problems with minor league thinking strategies. Where dichotomous thinkers take the easy route, critical thinkers spend the energy to consider multiple perspectives. That creates greatly expanded possibilities.

Ubiquitous Struggles

"Be kind; everyone you meet is fighting a hard battle." This quote is attributed to Ian McLaren (Quote Investigator, n.d.). Keeping this in mind will enrich your understanding of others. Experiences—battles won, lost, and ongoing—impact attitudes and perceptions. If someone in class is *very* committed to a position, the individual taking that strong position likely has a real connection to the issue that may be directly tied to their personal battle. Wise people and critical thinkers often disagree, yet still respect the position of others. Keep in mind that many individuals endure extra challenges to be sitting in the classroom. Following are just a few.

First-Generation College Students

First-generation students often struggle financially and may have guilt for being away from their families (Beresin, 2021). College often changes a person's perspectives as they learn from others. If you are a first-generation student, be mindful that these changes will, in all probability, impact relationships you have held with some family members and high school friends. It certainly did for me.

First-generation students also often find it challenging to fit in, might feel insecure, and may be confused about how the college system works. As a first-generation college student, for example, in my first semester I did not know that a person could drop a class. It was never an option in high school. In class discussions, first-generation students may not contribute much for fear of responding in a way that might reveal perceived shortcomings. These challenges add up: Ives and Castillo-Montoya (2020) reported that "only 56% [of first-generation college students] earn a baccalaureate degree within six years compared to 74% of students with a parent who graduated from college" (p. 139).

Research has shown that many students find relief talking to other first-generation students, and there are likely more first-generation students on campus than you think. Approximately one-third of college students are the first in their families to enter higher education (Ives & Castillo-Montoya, 2020). Most campuses now have free, confidential resources to help with the transition to college. If you are not a first-generation student, but know someone who is, help them out if you can.

Microaggressions

Students of color and those identified as "different" (e.g., a nonmajority gender identity, a learning disability, or different levels of physical ableness) face a constant barrage of *microaggressions*, which are subtle statements and behaviors, intentional or unintentional, that are hostile or derogatory. There are those who claim that victims of these statements are "overly sensitive," that nobody is really hurt by such comments, and that the victims need to realize that the comments are "only jokes." It would be bad enough if a person from a marginalized group heard disparaging comments only occasionally. Unfortunately, these statements and behaviors are often a constant, daily assault on the victim's sense of self. It is the accumulation of insults that makes microaggressions so insidious.

Examples of microaggressions (a not-at-all exhaustive list) include crossing the street to avoid an oncoming group of Black men on the sidewalk (implying that they are dangerous), complimenting a Japanese American student on their English (negating or refusing to acknowledge they are American), or using derogatory language to belittle particular groups. Microaggressions were initially defined as a form of discrimination toward ethnic minorities but they are equally damaging for any minoritized group, such as LGBTQIA+ individuals (Anzani et al., 2021).

With an increased awareness of what microaggressions are and the damage they can do, we need to call out and work to prevent such behavior. Inaction and silence support the dividing nature of microaggressions (Limbong, 2020). If you note someone committing a microaggression, and you feel safe, say something. Derald Sue and colleagues (2019) at Columbia University, in their article

"Disarming Racial Microaggressions," point out several ways you can help work against microaggressions. A person witnessing a microaggression can be a *deflector*, who directly puts an end to an act of aggression, acts as an ally, or educates the transgressor. Suppose a student sitting next to you in class points at the person in front of them and says, "We should get him to do our math homework. Chinese are good at math." To directly address this microaggression, you might say, "That is really inappropriate. It reinforces a stereotype." Be mindful that there are times when you may unintentionally perpetrate a microaggression. If this occurs and you realize it, or have it pointed out to you, be open to the correction, apologize, and explain you will work to do better next time.

Stereotype Threat

Steele and Aronson (1995) identified the concept of *stereotype threat*, in which one person is assumed to stand for their entire perceived group. Such assumptions often result in a negative impact on performance. For example, a Black student at a predominantly White school may be concerned that their academic performance will be interpreted as representative of all Black students. Research shows that when an individual believes that they are being singled out for their group identity (e.g., being a woman or Hispanic), it can increase stress to perform well, which often results in lower performance. Stricker and colleagues (2015) demonstrated stereotype threat in a study researching Black test-takers. When questions about race were asked prior to taking the test, test scores were lower than when such race questions were not asked (Stricker et al., 2015). This and other studies demonstrate that making a person from a marginalized group think about their race or ethnicity puts added pressure on them to do well. Stereotype threat and its implications on individual perspectives have been studied for many groups. Additional negative outcomes likely due to stereotype threat include Native Americans' lower grade point averages and hopelessness (Jaramillo et al., 2016), women's math performance (Spencer et al., 1999), and social interaction for individuals on the autism spectrum (Botha et al., 2020).

Implicit Bias

Implicit bias is an automatically triggered association between a social group and the perceived attributes of that group by third parties (Payne et al., 2018). Essentially, these are biases that you don't even know you have. Nearly everyone has some implicit biases. Payne and Vuletich from the University of North Carolina at Chapel Hill, along with Brown-Iannuzzi from the University of Kentucky, found that although self-reports of implicit bias have declined in recent years, cognitive tests show that this bias is still prevalent (Payne et al., 2018). Implicit bias can be directed at any group, for any reason, with very real and troubling results. For example, implicit bias can result in LGBTQIA+ students receiving poorer health care (Morris et al., 2019), social exclusion of individuals on the autism spectrum (University of Texas at Dallas, 2021), and unfair treatment of women and underrepresented groups in college engineering course teamwork (Isaac et al., 2023). Take careful note of your likely unintentional bias of others within a group, as that will impact how you interact with those individuals.

Generative Artificial Intelligence

Generative artificial intelligence (GenAI) is moving so fast that it is simply not possible to discuss in this book how it will impact individuals. One thing is certain: It will perpetuate substantial biases in multiple ways unless educated individuals work to change it. First, the material from which GenAI draws information is already biased, because the knowledge base was created by humans. If you are creating examples and a stereotype arises, adjust the prompt to correct the situation.

Biases in use of AI will also emerge based on resources. Those who have better resources will be able to better use GenAI. Those with access to thousands of GenAI programs (some at a cost) and the time and infrastructure (e.g., access to high-speed internet) to use it will be able to practice, hone their skills, and benefit from the products. For example, using GenAI to quiz you on organic principles will help you to learn the material faster than those who don't have ready access to computers and fast internet connections. AI will change the world—those who have the opportunity to use it have the power to direct *how.*

Summary of Biases: From Uneasy to Understanding

As you engage in higher education, you will have the opportunity to interact with individuals from a variety of groups. Your points of view will differ from theirs, and you will have to address preconceived ideas you have about some individuals. They will be prejudging you in the same way. We all have biases. The challenge is to work to mitigate those biases as much as possible.

As you interact with individuals who are different from you, it is perfectly normal to feel uncomfortable for a while. This is how the human brain is wired. We instinctively feel more comfortable when someone looks like us, acts like us, and likes what we like (Iacoboni, 2009). From an evolutionary and biological perspective, individuals different from you represent uncertainty, and uncertainty often makes people uncomfortable. However, if you are exposed to the same new types of situations repeatedly, the brain better understands what to expect, and with time the discomfort around the unfamiliar goes away (Martinez &

Derrick, 1996). The best way to feel comfortable with someone different from you is through direct interaction. The interactions will feel unfamiliar, and you may fear you will not understand them or that you might say something culturally insensitive. Communication is always the key. Across time you will find it easier and faster to understand and appreciate the perspectives of literally anyone. You will also find it easier and easier to ask an individual to help you to understand their position and their culture.

There is no harm in seeing differences among people. Differences are positive in many ways because they offer a diversity of perspectives and richness of life. The challenge is not to let those differences disparage or disadvantage anyone. As Maya Angelou said, "The truth is, no one of us can be free until everybody is free" (CNN, 2013, 1:09). That includes being free from bias.

Chapter Summary

College is an excellent place to have conversations with those who hold perspectives different from yours. Critical thinking requires that we avoid dichotomous thinking, as life has very few issues that allow for simple yes/no answers. As we engage in conversations in our courses, remember that everyone has a reason for their perspective and that everyone has a battle they have fought or are fighting, whether a temporary or ongoing circumstance, a difference in background from the majority, implicit biases, stereotype threat, or any combination of infinite personal factors. You will be uncomfortable at times in college, as will others in the room. With time and work—as you critically examine your preconceptions and biases (which we all have)—that discomfort will dissipate, and you will be left with new connections and a variety of perspectives rich with possibilities.

Discussion Questions

1 Describe one topic you have observed recently that is being presented dichotomously. Does this topic have two clear positions? What points of view or arguments can you think of on either side of the issue you've noted?
2 Over the period of a few days, watch for microaggressions (behavioral or verbal, made by others or yourself). Describe one of the microaggressions you observed and any potential impact.
3 If you had the opportunity to have a completely open and confidential conversation with an individual from a marginalized group to learn more about their perspective and experiences, who would you like to talk to, and what general topic would you desire to know more about? What resources, books, or articles can you access to begin educating yourself regarding this position?

References

Anzani, A., Sacchi, S., & Prunas, A. (2021). Microaggressions towards lesbian and transgender women: Biased information gathering when working alongside gender and sexual minorities. *Journal of Clinical Psychology*, *77*(9), 2027–2040. https://doi.org/10.1002/jclp.23140

Beresin, E. (2021, November 6). The challenge of first-generation college students. *Psychology Today*. https://www.psychologytoday.com/us/blog/inside-out-outside-in/202111/the-challenge-first-generation-college-students

Botha, M., Dibb, B., & Frost, D. M. (2020, October 6). "Autism is me": An investigation of how autistic individuals make sense of autism and stigma. *Disability and Society*. https://doi.org/10.1080/09687599.2020.1822782

CNN. (2013, August 28). *Angelou: "No one of us can be free until everybody is …"* [Video]. YouTube. https://www.youtube.com/watch?v=UxkTd6BFL1o

Iacoboni, M. (2009). Imitation, empathy, and mirror neurons. *Annual Review of Psychology*, *60*, 653–670. https://doi.org/10.1146/annurev.psych.60.110707.163604

Isaac, S., Kotluk, N., & Tormey, R. (2023). Educating engineering students to address bias and discrimination within their project teams. *Science and Engineering Ethics*, *29*, 6. https://doi.org/10.1007/s11948-022-00426-w

Ives, J., & Castillo-Montoya, M. (2020). First-generation college students as academic learners: A systematic review. *Review of Educational Research*, *90*(2), 139–178. https://doi.org/10.3102/0034654319899707

Jaramillo, J., Mello, Z. R., & Worrell, F. C. (2016). Ethnic identity, stereotype threat, and perceived discrimination among Native American adolescents. *Journal of Research on Adolescence*, *26*(4), 769–775. https://doi.org/10.1111/jora.12228

Limbong, A. (2020, June 9). *Microaggressions are a big deal: How to talk them out and when to walk away*. National Public Radio. https://www.npr.org/2020/06/08/872371063/microaggressions-are-a-big-deal-how-to-talk-them-out-and-when-to-walk-away

Martinez, J. L., & Derrick, B. E. (1996). Long-term potentiation and learning. *Annual Review of Psychology*, *47*(1), 173–203. https://doi.org/10.1146/annurev.psych.47.1.173

Morris, M., Cooper, R. L., Ramesh, A., Tabatabai, M., Arcury, T. A., Shinn, M., Im, W., Juarez, P., & Matthews-Juarez, P. (2019). Training to reduce LGBTQ-related bias among medical, nursing, and dental students and providers: A systematic review. *BMC Medical Education*, *19*(1), 325. https://doi.org/10.1186/s12909-019-1727-3

Payne, B. K., Vuletich, H. A., & Brown-Iannuzzi, J. L. (2018). Historical roots of implicit bias in slavery. *PNAS*, *116*(24), 11693–11698. https://doi.org/10.1073/pnas.1818816116

Quote Investigator. (n.d.). *Be kind; everyone you meet is fighting a hard battle*. https://quoteinvestigator.com/2010/06/29/be-kind/

Spencer, S. J., Steele, C. M., & Quinn, D. M. (1999). Stereotype threat and women's math performance. *Journal of Experimental Social Psychology*, *35*(1), 4–28. https://doi.org/10.1006/jesp.1998.1373

Steele, C. M., & Aronson, J. (1995). Stereotype threat and the intellectual test performance of African Americans. *Journal of Personality and Social Psychology*, *69*(5), 797–811. https://doi.org/10.1037//0022-3514.69.5.797

Stricker, L. J., Rock, D. A., & Bridgeman, B. (2015). *Stereotype threat, inquiring about test takers' race and gender, and performance on low-stakes tests in a large-scale assessment* (ETS Research Report No. RR-15-02). Educational Testing Service.

Sue, D. W., Alsaidi, S., Awad, M. N., Glaeser, E., Calle, C. Z., & Mendez, N. (2019). Disarming racial microaggressions: Microintervention strategies for targets, White allies, and bystanders. *American Psychologist*, *74*(1), 128–142. http://dx.doi.org/10.1037/amp0000296

University of Texas at Dallas. (2021, February 8). Reducing biases about autism may increase social inclusion, study finds. *ScienceDaily*. www.sciencedaily.com/releases/2021/02/210208085441.htm

2
ESTABLISHING YOURSELF
AS A LEARNER

In this chapter, we turn our attention to several things you can do to establish yourself as a learner. There is more to being a successful student than putting in time studying for exams and writing papers. Those are certainly important, but if you don't believe you can be successful, if you feel like an imposter, or lack the self-discipline to study when there is fun to be had, then it is unlikely that you will be a successful student. In this chapter, we will look at how you see yourself as a learner and what you can do to establish a more solid foundation from which you can learn nearly anything.

Self-Regulation

Self-regulation is the process that helps you meet your personal goals (Inzlicht et al., 2021). Sometimes what you want to do and what is the best for you are the same. When they aren't, in order to be successful, you will need to regulate your behavior and choose what is most appropriate.

The first year of college allows students a lot of freedom that was likely not available just a few months prior. Just as in high school, there will be fun activities, time spent lazing around, and periods of hard work. The primary difference is that instead of being told when to do homework, what to eat, and when to stop playing video games, students make their own decisions. Unfortunately, too many students make the wrong decision. Nearly one out of every three students drops out of college before sophomore year (Hanson, 2021). Many of those who don't succeed likely struggled with self-regulation.

Self-regulation requires an individual to identify a target outcome, plan how to reach the target, and stick to the planned behavior until the target outcome

DOI: 10.4324/9781003499176-3

is reached. For example, suppose you make a goal to be on the dean's list your first year at college. You decide to study for 1 hour for each of your four classes every day, including Saturday, although you plan to take Sunday off to relax and do something fun. During the fourth week of the semester, a few of your friends tell you Thursday afternoon that Friday at 3:00 p.m. they are planning a road trip: They'll take turns driving through the night Friday evening, do some sightseeing Saturday, see a concert Saturday evening, and then drive back to campus on Sunday. The trip and the concert sound amazing. The problem is that you have two exams on Monday. You may start to rationalize that you can study more Sunday evening and that even if your grades drop a bit, you can get them back up later in the semester. It will take a lot of self-regulation to turn down a trip that sounds fun and stick to your study plan. Establishing a productive self-regulation system is critical in the first semester of college. After your first year, the self-regulation processes you establish become habits for success, which you can continue to adjust, adapt, and alter as needed.

———◆———

Study Tip 2.1: Start as small as necessary, but develop a habit of completing whatever goal you set.

———◆———

Managing Emotions

Self-regulation of emotions is a lifelong, needed skill that we typically are taught as children.

As adults, some individuals, find self-regulation challenging. Emotion is part of the limbic system, the oldest and most primitive part of the brain. Emotions can emerge and escalate without the individual even knowing why they feel that way or at least why they feel that intensely. Failure to regulate emotion can be problematic when it comes to learning. I have seen students get frustrated with faculty, be unable to regulate their emotions, and devolve into aggressive shouting. That never ends well.

It is important to recognize when frustration is building and manage the situation. Exercise is a great long-term help with managing emotions in stressful situations (Oaten & Cheng, 2006), but in the short term, try deep breathing or literally step away for a few minutes, if possible. Temperament is a big part of self-regulation. If a person has an aggressive or anxious temperament, for example, it takes more effort to demonstrate emotional self-regulation (Rothbart, 1981). This means that managing emotions is easier for some people than it is for others. However, society does not make allowances based on temperament; everyone is expected to manage emotions appropriately.

Self-Efficacy

Self-efficacy is the extent to which you believe you can be successful at a given task (Bandura, 1997). This becomes particularly important when faced with something that is challenging. It is much easier to be successful if you believe you have the ability to be successful.

According to Bandura, the following four major influences determine our level of self-efficacy and, as a result, the extent to which we are successful.

Performance Outcomes

If you are asked to do something new that is a bit challenging, it is helpful to compare this task to similar tasks you have done. If you have already successfully done something very similar (had a successful performance outcome), you will be more likely to believe that this new task is also possible (high self-efficacy). If this new task is nothing like anything you have done before, or like something which you previously tried and failed (a nonexistent or negative performance outcome), you are likely to be less confident in your ability to complete it (low self-efficacy). When you find yourself struggling to complete a task, think about similar tasks you have done in the past.

Vicarious Experiences

Watching others engage in a behavior impacts your self-efficacy, particularly if you identify with the person completing the behavior (e.g., siblings, parents, friends, teachers, classmates, and even celebrities). If a person with whom you identify is able to accomplish a task, you are motivated to try. Think of the number of times a sibling, friend, or teacher did something to show you how it could be done or the number of times you tried a dance you saw demonstrated on TikTok. Of course, if the person you watch fails, it may well convince you that you won't be able to successfully accomplish the task (lowered self-efficacy).

Study Tip 2.2: Seeing a task being done correctly builds your self-efficacy. If you don't know how to do something, ask someone to show you, so you can see someone be successful at the task.

Verbal Persuasion

Another impact on your potential success is what it is said to you during the attempt. The phrase, "Come on, I know you can do it," is a positive *verbal persuasion*. In teaching statistics, I regularly encourage my students this way. Unfortunately, negative verbal persuasion also be detrimental to self-efficacy. Imagine the self-efficacy of a 13-year-old girl in middle school when a biology teacher tells her she is struggling in class because girls are not good at science. As reprehensible as that is to imagine, the biology example happened to someone in my family just a few years ago. Verbal persuasion can also be less obvious, such as the "chilly climate," where women are not treated as well as men in the classroom, particularly in fields related to science, technology, engineering, and math (STEM). Verbal persuasion is also found with microaggressions, where individuals from underrepresented groups are told via implied, offhand, and (often) unintentionally cruel statements they cannot be successful because of who they are (Walton et al., 2015).

Physiological Feedback

Performing any action (e.g., waiting for your final exam to start, speaking to your professor for the first time, giving a presentation) often results in *physiological (bodily) feedback* (e.g., racing heart, sweaty palms, nausea). How you interpret those feelings will impact your self-efficacy. Even though I have given a lot of presentations, I still feel my heart rate speed up, my mouth gets dry, and my stomach feels uneasy just before I start. If I interpret those sensations as standard nerves before a presentation and remind myself that feeling a bit nervous makes a person a better presenter, then my self-efficacy increases. However, if I interpret those feelings as insecurity because I feel unprepared, my self-efficacy may decline.

Self-efficacy has a significant impact on behavior. People are much more likely to put forth energy toward a task when they are reasonably confident of success. Fencl and Scheel (2005) found that just about any teaching method that included student participation increased self-efficacy. So, participate in class when collaborative and engaged learning techniques like small groups, Think-Pair-Share, and so on are used. Avoid negative talk, as it can lower your self-efficacy, and watch good role models do well. These things can help you learn in harmony with your brain.

Imposter Syndrome

Clance and Imes (1978), while at Georgia State University, first described imposter syndrome after interviewing more than 150 successful women. Many of these women did not perceive themselves as successful, despite outstanding achievements, high praise, and professional recognition. Many of these women reported feeling like "imposters."

Imposter syndrome remains common, with as many as 70% of all adults reporting that they experienced feelings of being an imposter at least once (Gravois, 2007). The challenge is that individuals are often *not* at the inferior level they feel they are. For example, within our society, women are often socialized to be more nurturing, gentle, and nonconfrontational than are men. As a result, women are more likely than men to present suggested changes and new ideas as questions rather than making statement of how things should be done (Johnson, 2017). Suppose Alice has an idea as to the direction a new initiative should take. During a team meeting she says, "With what we know, June seems a reasonable time to start. Does that make sense to the group?" Alice may know the best course of action, but to get buy-in from the group she knows to use questions. However, questions such as this may be perceived by team members as Alice being uncertain and either looking for answers or second-guessing herself. If Alice later is uncertain as to how things are going and says she feels like an imposter, others on the team may think, "Well, she does tend to shy away from making tough decisions." This may create or reinforce feelings of being an imposter that are nothing more than a strategy of leading with a bit of uncertainty as to whether the course of action is the best.

Individuals from marginalized backgrounds are constantly questioned about their abilities and contributions relative to others (Tulshyan & Burey, 2021). These individuals are put into a position where they must always be cautious to not "offend" anyone. Being assertive or questioning those in established positions is usually seen as hostility from those members. After some time, those in the majority see someone in the marginalized group as uncertain, unwilling to commit to a course of action, and unwilling to defend their work. As a result, those in the marginalized group may need to constantly justify their knowledge and experience, and often begin to question their own expertise.

Imposter syndrome has many negative implications. Those with imposter syndrome are more likely to have stress, anxiety, and depression, and are more likely to drop out of college (Chrousos & Mentis, 2020). Imposter syndrome is found at much higher rates for underrepresented and marginalized groups (e.g., women, LGBTQIA+, Latinx, etc.), individuals who often slip through the cracks of higher education. Thus, understanding and combatting imposter syndrome is critical. As Kar (2021) notes, nearly everyone is concerned at times that they are imposters. The point is that if you feel nervous or uncertain or wonder "What on earth am I doing here?" you are experiencing life very much as everyone else does. There is no need to question your overall ability or justify why you are part of the group. These outmoded and incorrect perceptions are what perpetuate stereotypes and injustices. Individuals from the majority group also make mistakes and lack knowledge in some areas, but their lapses tend to be attributed to the difficulty of the situation. In contrast, those from underrepresented and marginalized groups in the same situation are accused of being unprepared or incompetent. It is time to stop the double standard.

Learned Optimism

In 1990, Martin Seligman started a movement called learned optimism. With this effort, Seligman launched the new area of positive psychology and published a book called *Learned Optimism: How to Change Your Mind and Your Life*. Much of psychology is all about pinpointing what is wrong and fixing it. In positive psychology, one focuses on a person's assets and builds on them (Seligman, 1990, 2018).

Researchers began investigating ways to help individuals instill optimism, primarily by developing favorable expectancies for the future (Carver & Scheier, 2014) and identify ways to think about the causes of optimism (Seligman, 2018). This area was the original AI, as in appreciative inquiry. Appreciative inquiry is a strengths-based approach; instead of trying to fix what you are doing wrong, focus on what you do best (Walker, 2023). This is easy to apply to your learning success. If you are good at bringing people together and organizing efforts, then a viable way to prepare for exams is to form study groups. If, on the other hand, you are good at summarizing material and sticking to a schedule, then it may be better for you to study with one other similar person or perhaps learn material on your own and then review and practice with a small group.

The overarching concept is to identify what you do well and work from your strengths. Individuals who focus on optimism have many positive outcomes, such as lower stress, better health, and lower blood pressure.

Chapter Summary

Self-regulation is an essential aspect of learning, as it includes setting a course of action and following that course. This is an important component of impulse control and reaching goals. Self-regulation interacts with many of the other concepts presented in this book, including metacognition, self-efficacy, procrastination, and cognitive load. These concepts by no means work in isolation. A critical area of self-regulation is emotional control. Our society, from the classroom to the supermarket, is based on being able to control one's emotions and behaving within certain parameters in public.

Along with self-regulation, self-efficacy is exceedingly important when it comes to learning. Self-efficacy pertains to the extent to which a person believes they can be successful at a task and is an integral part of motivation. Imposter syndrome impacts academic performance, but may have as much to do with social demands that place individuals into situations where they question their own expertise as with any individual factors. Imposter syndrome is not a personal issue; it is a cultural and societal issue and must be addressed. Another area in which to better understand yourself as a learner is learned optimism. The extent to which you successfully navigate certain circumstances may well be due to learning how to proactively and positively impact future behavior.

Discussion Questions

1 Being at college can bring about many emotions: missing home, navigating roommate interactions, increased scholarly expectations, and a host of other experiences and demands. What positive coping skills have you used? What maladaptive coping skills have you used? To what extent do you feel you are successful in managing your emotions?

2 Describe one area in which you have low self-efficacy and one area where your self-efficacy is relatively high. List what interactions led you to experience the high self-efficacy. Then explain what you could do to help raise your self-efficacy in the first area (consider areas of performance outcome, vicarious experience, verbal persuasion, and physiological feedback).

3 Research indicates that nearly 70% of adults experience imposter syndrome at some point (Gravois, 2007). Have you ever experienced imposter syndrome? With the knowledge you have gained from this chapter, how might you think differently about similar situations in the future?

References

Bandura, A. (1997). *Self-efficacy: The exercise of control*. W. H. Freeman/Times Books/ Henry Holt.

Carver, C. S., & Scheier, M. F. (2014). Dispositional optimism. *Trends in Cognitive Sciences, 18*(6), 293–299. https://doi.org/10.1016/j.tics.2014.02.003

Chrousos, G. P., & Mentis, A.-F. A. (2020). Imposter syndrome threatens diversity. *Science, 367*(6479), 749–750. https://doi.org/10.1126/science.aba8039

Clance, P. R., & Imes, S. A. (1978). The impostor phenomenon in high achieving women: Dynamics and therapeutic intervention. *Psychotherapy: Theory, Research, and Practice, 15*(3), 241–247. https://doi.org/10.1037/h0086006

Fencl, H., & Scheel, K. (2005). Research and teaching: Engaging students–an examination of the effects of teaching strategies on self-efficacy and course in a nonmajors physics course. *Journal of College Science Teaching, 35*(1), 20–24. https://my.nsta.org/ resource/?id=10.2505/4/jcst05_035_01_20

Gravois, J. (2007, November 9). You're not fooling anyone. *The Chronicle of Higher Education, 54*(11), A1. https://www.chronicle.com/article/youre-not-fooling-anyone/

Hanson, M. (2021). *College dropout rates*. Education Data Initiative. https://educationdata. org/college-dropout-rates

Inzlicht, M., Werner, K. M., Briskin, J. L., & Roberts, B. W. (2021). Integrating models of self-regulation. *Annual Review of Psychology, 72*(1), 319–345. https://doi.org/10.1146/annurev-psych-061020-105721

Johnson, S. K. (2017, August 17). What the science actually says about gender gaps in the workplace. *Harvard Business Review*. https://hbr.org/2017/08/what-the-science-actually-says-about-gender-gaps-in-the-workplace

Kar, P. (2021). Partha Kar: Imposter syndrome is no cause for shame. *BMJ: British Medical Journal (Online)*, 373. http://dx.doi.org/10.1136/bmj.n1387

Oaten, M., & Cheng, K. (2006). Longitudinal gains in self-regulation from regular physical exercise. *British Journal of Health Psychology, 11*(4), 717–733. https://doi.org/10.1348/135910706X96481

Rothbart, M. K. (1981). Measurement of temperament in infancy. *Child Development, 52*(2), 569–578. https://doi.org/10.2307/1129176

Seligman, M. E. P. (1990). *Learned optimism: How to change your mind and your life*. Random House.

Seligman, M. E. P. (2018). *The hope circuit: A psychologist's journey from helplessness to optimism*. PublicAffairs.

Tulshyan, R., & Burey, J. A. (2021, February 11). Stop telling women they have imposter syndrome. *Harvard Business Review*. https://hbr.org/2021/02/stop-telling-women-they-have-imposter-syndrome

Walker, K. D. (2023). Appreciative inquiry. In J. M. Okoko, S. Tunison, & K. D. Walker (Eds.), *Varieties of qualitative research methods* (pp. 29–33). Springer. https://doi.org/10.1007/978-3-031-04394-9_5

Walton, G. M., Logel, C., Peach, J. M., Spencer, S. J., & Zanna, M. P. (2015). Two brief interventions to mitigate a "chilly climate" transform women's experience, relationships, and achievement in engineering. *Journal of Educational Psychology, 107*(2), 468–485. https://doi.org/10.1037/a0037461

3

DEVELOPING YOUR
LEARNING STRATEGY

When I started at college, my "strategy" was to get good grades. I didn't get good grades … and it turned out that my plan wasn't a strategy. Fortunately, in my second semester, I started to figure out how to develop a solid learning strategy, and that helped keep me in college. In this chapter, we look at strategies to support success, include setting goals, building schedules, setting up to-do lists, being organized, and communicating with faculty. It won't take you much time at all to start thinking strategy, and the results have enormous potential.

Setting Goals

A *goal* is basically a desired result—what you want. You likely set vague goals all the time, such as wanting to get a good grade in psychology, find a better job, or get a decent night of sleep once in a while. Studies clearly and consistently show that setting specific and challenging goals results in better performance and greater feelings of achievement than setting goals that are easy, unobtainable, or nonexistent (e.g., Locke & Latham, 2006). It is best to stay away from goals that are too ambitious (e.g., get 100% on my next test) or too ambiguous (e.g., get a good grade in psychology).

Set SMART Goals

The acronym SMART is frequently used to remind individuals of the components of a well-written goal: Specific, Measurable, Achievable, Relevant, and Timely. A quick web search will result in many options for resources regarding

DOI: 10.4324/9781003499176-4

how to write effective SMART goals (and other types of goals) in a variety of settings (e.g., Bird et al., 2024; Martins, 2021).

The SMART framework will help you write specific goals at multiple levels: course, semester, year, and even for graduation. Use shorter goals to stay motivated and longer goals to keep focused across time.

Study Tip 3.1: Practice setting one SMART goal for each individual study session. With practice, it will become faster and easier to set quick goals.

Specific. Your goal needs to be specific and clearly defined so you know exactly what you are striving to accomplish. "Do well" in your class this semester is too vague. Will the meaning of "do well" shift during the semester? A specific goal might be to earn enough points to maintain at least a B – average in the course.

Measurable. Set goals that are objective and quantifiable. A goal of "exercise more" is not quantifiable. Your "more" may be very different than mine. A measurable goal would be to walk at least 10,000 steps every day.

Achievable. You must be able to *reach* the goal. If you are averaging a 65% in your class going into the final, a goal of "score 100% on the comprehensive final exam" is not achievable. An ideal goal is about 90% of the estimated level of the best expected outcome possible (Locke & Latham, 2002). In this case, a goal of 75% might be best.

Relevant. Your goal should mean something to you. When I taught behavior modification, I could always tell when people wanted to stop smoking for themselves or the health of a family member versus doing it because someone said they should. Those who wanted it for themselves and their family had a higher success rate.

Timely. Your goal should balance short-term gratification with long-term impact. In other words, you should have enough time to really achieve something, but it shouldn't be so far in the future that you lose interest along the way. For example, go to the museum twice before the end of the semester.

Break Large Goals Into Smaller Goals

Long-term, large goals provide a great sense of accomplishment but can be overwhelming on a day-to-day basis. For example, imagine that you set the following SMART goal: Get a 3.0 GPA for fall semester. That is specific, measurable, attainable, relevant, and time bound, but it will take effort in many areas to achieve. To have a better chance of success, create subgoals (e.g., determining the number of hours you will study each day, setting up study groups, or increasing the use of metacognitive strategies) that can be accomplished relatively quickly to provide motivation and feedback to long-term, larger goals (Tabachnick et al., 2008). It is good to have both overall goals and subgoals, so you can see where you are going *and* how to get there (Latham & Brown, 2006).

Build Your Schedule

With goals in place, the next step is to manage the tasks necessary to achieve them. Use your course syllabus to map out your academic responsibilities, and then add your class, family, and work obligations to your schedule or calendar.

I recognize the burden many of you face as you juggle multiple responsibilities. Perna and Odle (2020) reported, via the National Center for Educational Statistics, that 27% of full-time students and 71% of part-time students work 20 or more hours per week. In that same article, the authors presented data from the U.S. Department of Education showing that students from historically underserved groups, independent students, and students who are single parents with a dependent child are particularly likely to work long hours in addition to their academic responsibilities. I worked 30 hours per week or more for much of my undergraduate program, and two jobs each summer. I understand the stress this creates. The busier you are, the more value there is for a well-planned schedule manage your limited time.

The following are some tips to build your schedule:

- Put all exams, quizzes, assignments, or other class deadlines from each course syllabus on your calendar. Assume everything will go well, *and* schedule extra time for when it doesn't.
- Map out exactly when you intend to study (and where). Treat those study blocks like attending a meeting or a shift at work.
- Consider varying your study spaces to keep yourself engaged (Brooks, 2019).
- Schedule time for yourself, just like meetings, classes, or study blocks. If you need "you time" to be healthier and cognitively sharp, make it a priority.
- Try to reserve 1 hour every day in case something (errands, drafting an outline, picking up the kids, unexpected wait at office hours) takes longer than expected. If everything goes as planned, enjoy the luxury of some unanticipated "you time"!
- Learn when to say "no" and when to say "yes." If you keep a good calendar, you will know if time exists to take on a task. If it doesn't, explain that you are at capacity, but that you appreciate being asked and would appreciate being considered for future opportunities.

Manage Your Schedule

Once built, it can be challenging to manage your schedule. There are many systems out there, and a key component is the to-do list. There are many resources for setting up and managing a to-do list. I manage my to-do list using the free version of http://Todoist.com. That is one that works for me. Find a system that works best for *you* (Pot, 2021). You may be tempted to have different systems to manage your schedule. It is best to have one system. As an FYI, sticky notes posted all over your living space may be good reminders, but that is not a schedule management system.

Organization

Have you ever noticed that some people have a very organized workspace and computer desktop, whereas others have piles of papers all over their workspace and can't find anything on their computer desktop? I am convinced it is because the person with a clean work area considers a task "done" only when the product of the task (paper, flashcards, spreadsheet) is filed, whereas the person with piles everywhere considers the task done when they hit the Send key. The second individual doesn't file the completed assignment in a drawer, their hard drive, the cloud, or anywhere else. When you finish your term paper and email it to your professor, don't cross the task off your to-do list until you take 2 more minutes to save the material where you can find it later—maybe something like: Documents → 2023 Fall Semester → PSYCH 101 → Final Paper → COMPLETE. Don't just trust that you'll remember when you sent an email or that you sent an email at all. Think of it this way: Is dinner done when you finish eating or when the dishes are washed and everything is thrown or put away? When you next visit a friend's apartment or look at their laptop, see if you can tell when they think a task is "done."

Effective Communication Patterns

As a first-generation college student, I had no idea how to address a faculty member or even at times what to say. When I started my first faculty position, I also quickly noticed that students from different backgrounds have different skill sets in the area of communication strategies. Being an effective communicator is another area that you can improve with a bit of work and a few resources.

Be an Active Listener

When speaking with a professor, *listen actively* (Brownlee, 2020). Monitor your thoughts to ensure that you are not thinking of something else while your professor, peer, or colleague is talking. I admit that my mind often wanders while others are talking. There are times we must make a concerted effort to attend to the conversation at hand. This is a natural human condition (and especially difficult for people with ADHD), but it's important to make the effort.

Confirm you are understanding by summarizing any significant points that your professor covered in the conversation. For example, imagine you are at your professor's office hours to talk about choosing your paper topic. You might finish the conversation by asking the professor if you can summarize what was discussed to be sure you have it correct. Doing this is not wasting the faculty member's time. It will only take about 10–15 seconds, and your professor will appreciate that you want to get it right.

I suspect it goes without saying, but it's too important not to say it: Never multitask while conversing with a professor. If you would like to take notes, that is fine. Just ask first, "Is it okay if I take notes on my phone/laptop/planner?" Doing so makes it clear to your professor that you are attending to the conversation, and not ignoring the professor and doing something else. Finally, if you are confused or uncertain about anything, ask for clarification. It is much better to ask than to get something wrong in an assignment. Students will sometimes assure faculty that they understand, because they are embarrassed that they are lost or are nervous and want to escape the conversation. Please ask: Faculty want you to be successful.

How to Address Faculty

It can be confusing to move from high school, where nearly everyone is Mr. or Ms., to a world of professors, doctors, adjuncts, teaching assistants (TAs), and instructors. However, there are straightforward and consistent rules, whether you are at a university, college, community/technical college, or anywhere else in higher ed. You will likely be told how to address your professor or TA on the first day of class or in the first online module. Use what they indicate is their preference, even if it is a bit uncomfortable for you at first. If you are not told what to call them, it's safest to go with "Professor," particularly if they have "professor" anywhere in their title, including assistant and associate professors. Adjunct faculty members and instructors (sometimes known as *contingent faculty*) are hired for set periods of time. These individuals may also all be called "professor." They will let you know if they prefer something else. If you know the faculty member has a doctorate (PhD, EdD, PsyD, PharmD, MD, etc.), you can call them "Dr. Last Name." If you don't know how to pronounce their name, ask them or find out from the department office professional. This isn't being rude—it's being respectful of their name.

In general, do not call faculty members "Mr." or "Mrs." unless they specifically tell you to do so. One exception is graduate teaching assistants (GTAs).

They can be called "Mr.," "Ms.," or "Mx." (pronounced mix), unless they have completed their doctorate, in which case it is appropriate to call them "Dr." If you are unsure, just ask. By the way, if our paths should happen to cross, call me Dr. Zakrajsek (you can ask me how to pronounce it), Dr. Z, or Todd, whichever you find most comfortable.

Make Use of Office Hours

Office hours are times set aside for students to access their faculty. This time is for you, so you don't ever need to start by saying, "I'm sorry to bother you." It is fine to start with "Do you have a few minutes?" Also, if a professor is working, they are just making good use of time until you stop by; they are not too busy for you. Once a student came to my office hour and let me know he had been by on two other occasions, but I had been on my computer, so he left. If your professor is working, simply knock.

If none of the times listed as office hours work for your schedule, it is appropriate to ask your professor if you can schedule another time to meet, in person, on the phone, or over videoconference (e.g., Zoom, Teams, Meet).

Study Tip 3.2: Stop by during an office hour and ask your professor a question or just say "hi." Don't take too much time. The idea is to be comfortable stopping by and also to make sure your professor knows you care about the class.

Emails to Faculty

Many faculty use email as a major communication platform. Be friendly, but also professional. Take a few minutes and read the blog post accessed from Figure 3.1 by Laura Portwood-Stacer (2016).

Portwood-Stacer does an excellent job of covering the basics. Here are a few additional tips:

- Send your email from your college email account so your professor's spam filter doesn't block it.
- Keep personal information to a minimum. If you missed a class and want to let the professor know, you can simply say that you could not attend class and note that you can provide details if needed. Most faculty members will not ask for them, but some do.

Retrieved from https://medium.com/@lportwoodstacer/how-to-email-your-professor-without-being-annoying-af-cf64ae0e4087

FIGURE 3.1   QR Code for "How to Email Your Professor (Without Being Annoying AF)."

Source: Portwood-Stacer (2016).

- Use professional verbiage.

  - Write words out in full.
  - Use conventional spellings.
  - Use emojis, memes, or gifs sparingly.

- Close with "Thank you," and your full name.

Finally, be sure to include the course you are in and the time the class meets somewhere in the email. One semester I taught three introductory psychology classes with 200 students each, a history of psychology class, and a course on human learning. A student sent me an email that said, "I am sorry about missing class today. Is there anything I should read to be ready for class on Wednesday?" The email was signed from Chris. I had multiple Chris's in each class that semester. In the end I emailed Chris to get clarification. It took only a few extra minutes, but with nearly 700 students, a few "extra-minute" tasks can quickly add up to hours.

Making Requests

Sometimes you'll need to miss class, make up an exam, or turn in an assignment late. Check the syllabus carefully and learn as much as you can about the course policies before making a request. If the syllabus clearly states there are no extensions or makeup exams, acknowledge that you have read the syllabus's policy about extensions, have an incredibly good reason why you need one anyway, and be prepared for a "no."

The following are the three big considerations when you make a request of a professor:

1 Time. Some requests can be very time consuming. I have written hundreds of reference letters for students. I don't think students realize it takes about an hour to an hour and a half to do each one, which I often ended up doing in the evenings or on weekends.

2 Fairness. If you ask for an extension regarding a paper deadline, your professor needs to offer that to others in the class. Additionally, moving a due date means the time to return the assignments also moves.

3 Respect. Remember, you are essentially asking for a favor (even if you feel that you have an exceptional reason). Keep the exchange respectful. A student once left me a voicemail of "Hey, this is Morgan. I couldn't make it to the exam yesterday. Give me a call, and we'll schedule a makeup." My syllabus clearly stated that I would give a makeup exam to anyone who needed it, *if* I was notified in advance, so that I could schedule all makeup exams at once. Morgan called after the exam, didn't give a reason, and didn't even leave a way to get in touch. Be considerate with messages. Don't be like Morgan.

Chapter Summary

Setting goals helps most individuals to survive and, at times, thrive. Use the SMART framework to ensure your goals are specific, measurable, achievable, relevant, and timely. Include subgoals in your big goals so you get regular bursts of achievement and stay motivated.

To manage your responsibilities, use a single calendar system, maintain a to-do list, and organize work as it is completed. College is also a time to develop and strengthen professional communication. When talking to professors, develop active learning strategies to ensure comprehension and address professors using the appropriate professional title. Use office hours or make an appointment to clarify information or ask questions. Always check the syllabus before making any requests. Finally, in setting goals, interacting with your professors, and meeting the course requirements, there will be periodic setbacks. That happens to everyone. It happened to me several times. Through that rollercoaster, keep the big picture in mind and focus on your ultimate goal for attending college.

Discussion Questions

1 Load the deadlines and expected time to work on classes into your calendar. How busy is the semester going to be for you? What concerns you most about your calendar, schedule, and maintaining this system?

2 What system do you use or will you use for a to-do list? Explain why you use this system or why you might switch.

3 Read through each of your syllabi. Note what requests you can and cannot make based on professors' policies. Explain briefly why you think your professors have the policies they do for attendance, paper deadlines, exam make-ups, and so on.

References

Bird, M. D., Swann, C., & Jackman, P. C. (2024). The what, why, and how of goal setting: A review of the goal-setting process in applied sport psychology practice. *Journal of Applied Sport Psychology, 36*(1), 75–97. https://doi.org/10.1080/10413200.2023.2185699

Brooks, A. (2019, February 25). 7 tips to create the perfect study environment for you. *Rasmussen University College Life Blog.* https://www.rasmussen.edu/student-experience/college-life/study-environment-tips/

Brownlee, D. (2020, August 6). Are you really listening or just waiting to talk? There's a difference. *Forbes.* https://www.forbes.com/sites/danabrownlee/2020/08/06/are-you-really-listening-or-just-waiting-to-talk-theres-a-difference/?sh=77b698b76085

Latham, G. P., & Brown, T. C. (2006). The effect of learning, distal, and proximal goals on MBA self-efficacy and satisfaction. *Applied Psychology: An International Review, 55*(4), 6060–6123. https://doi.org/10.1002/job.70

Locke, E. A., & Latham, G. P. (2002). Building a practically useful theory of goal setting and task motivation: A 35-year odyssey. *American Psychologist, 57*(9), 705–717. https://doi.org/10.1037//0003-066X.57.9.705

Locke, E. A., & Latham, G. P. (2006). New directions in goal-setting theory. *Current Directions in Psychological Science, 15*(5), 265–268. https://doi.org/10.1111/j.1467-8721.2006.00449.x

Martins, J. (2021, January 8). Write better SMART goals with these tips and examples. *Asana.* https://asana.com/resources/smart-goals

Perna, L. W., & Odle, T. K. (2020). Recognizing the reality of working college students: Minimizing the harm and maximizing the benefits of work. *Academe.* https://www.aaup.org/article/recognizing-reality-working-college-students#.YiVJphNKhBw

Portwood-Stacer, L. (2016, April 26). How to email your professor (without being annoying AF). *Medium.* https://medium.com/@lportwoodstacer/how-to-email-your-professor-without-being-annoying-af-cf64ae0e4087

Pot, J. (2021, November 16). The 8 best to do list apps of 2022. *Zapier.* https://zapier.com/blog/best-todo-list-apps/

Tabachnick, S. E., Miller, R. B., & Relyea, G. E. (2008). The relationships among students' future-oriented goals and subgoals, perceived task instrumentality, and task-oriented self-regulation strategies in an academic environment. *Journal of Educational Psychology, 100*(3), 629–642. https://doi.org/10.1037/0022-0663.100.3.629

PART 2
Build Your Foundation

4

IMPROVING THE LEARNING PROCESS

It wasn't until I flunked a few exams in college that I first learned about learning. I had been a very good high school student; I studied some, and was always on the honor roll. In college, that changed. I got scores much lower than I had ever seen before even though I was studying more. I was in the process of dropping out of college when Dr. Sawyer, my psychology professor, told me about learning how to learn. Much of this chapter is based on what I learned while I was an undergraduate, which kept me in college with consistent grades of As and Bs. I still had to work more for grades than I had to in high school, but at least I knew how to do it more efficiently and effectively.

Why do we need to learn how to learn? For much of our lives, we function on a kind of autopilot, which keeps us from being overwhelmed by, well, everything. The next time you walk somewhere, notice all the things you probably never think about while moving forward on foot. You likely don't think about shifting your weight for each step, what you do with your arms, or how much you lean when walking around a corner. Running on autopilot with minimal attention works well to keep things going as they are. However, most of us were never taught in school that to learn something new you must *turn off* autopilot and *focus* on the specific skill you wish to learn or enhance. Once the new information or skill is learned and practiced, you will be able to shift back to autopilot, except on a whole new level.

Learning About Learning

You are already very good at learning. You have been learning all your life. You learn where and how to get carryout food, which of your friends can keep a secret, and to look before crossing a road. Most of the learning you have done is

DOI: 10.4324/9781003499176-6

just part of your everyday life. Learning in school probably looks very different to you, and likely harder than learning while living. The secret is that the fundamental principles are the same. Once you see that, although most learning won't be easy—because all learning takes some work—it will likely be much easier.

Few realize how much they have going for them when it comes to learning. The human brain has amazing capabilities. Even though the average human brain is only about the size of your two fists put together, it has approximately 86 billion neurons (Azevedo et al., 2009). To get an idea of how big this number is, tap a finger on a surface near you, at the pace of one tap per second. To get to 86 billion, you would need to do that for just a bit over 2,700 years. That would be like starting to tap in 700 B.C. and finishing right about now. That is a lot of neurons, and the neurons in your brain are used for all learning. With that many neurons and the right strategies, you can learn just about anything.

Although our brains can hold a nearly endless amount of information, learning is not instantaneous. That is by design, so we don't overload our brains. Learning something new must be worth the space that information will occupy, so our brains are designed to make us work for it a bit. That means all humans are a bit slow at learning new things. What determines how much we can learn at any given time? The answer is cognitive load.

Managing Cognitive Load

Cognitive load refers to the amount of information that can be processed at any given moment (Sweller, 1988). Imagine a highway; everything flows along until there are too many cars, at which point a traffic jam occurs. Our neurons are like that highway, and information is like the cars. Once we max out cognitive load, we have a mental traffic jam. If you are trying to study with maxed out cognitive load (too much information coming in), you are wasting your time. Everyone maxes out at times, even experts. For an example of too much cognitive load, think of a time you were reading challenging material and people started a conversation nearby. The combination of the challenging material and the conversation is enough to cause a cognitive traffic jam. It would be a waste of time to keep trying to read. Either the person reading must relocate or the conversation has to move. Recognizing when there is too much cognitive load and knowing to make adjustments will make you a more effective and more efficient learner. There are only three types of cognitive load: intrinsic, extraneous, and germane (Sweller et al., 1988). Once you understand these, you will be learning in harmony with your brain.

Intrinsic Load

Intrinsic cognitive load is the complexity that naturally occurs in any given task. Intrinsic means innate or essential, simply "the way something is." Reading in a language you are just learning is always more difficult than reading in your first language. Organic chemistry is more challenging than introductory mathematics.

With a bit of practice, you will become better and better at estimating your intrinsic load for a task, which will help you structure your study or work time. If you are assigned to read an easy chapter from a novel and are told only to get a gist of the story, that's a low intrinsic load task; you can plan to do that when you are tired or in a busy place like a break at work. Studying for an exam in a challenging course is high intrinsic load, so you'll need to schedule focused study time in a quiet place. Taking just a few minutes to determine a task's intrinsic load will help make your study time more efficient.

Extraneous Load

The second type of cognitive load is *extraneous load*. Extraneous means irrelevant or unrelated. These are distractions in your environment that take cognitive energy but do not help with your assigned task. You often have control over extraneous load. Minimizing extraneous load, when possible, is key to making study time effective because you will have more mental energy to allocate to your academic work. If you get good at this, you should be able to learn more content than you have in the past, and likely in less time. Try something right now. Take a few seconds to see what extraneous load exists in your environment. If there is none, that is fantastic. However, if the TV is on, you are texting periodically, or roommates are having a debate about dorm food, that is all extraneous load. Music is often considered extraneous load, even classical music (Kumaradevan et al., 2021). However, if you find silence unsettling or if you can't get away from the sounds of others, try using an ambient music app or find "music to study by" from an app, YouTube, or a streaming channel. Now you know the psychological rationale for finding a quiet, comfortable place to study. It reduces extraneous cognitive load, which increases the cognitive energy you can allocate to your work.

Another source of extraneous load is smartphones. I know it is challenging, but if you put your phone away during class or when studying (if studying set a timer for 1 hour), stop thinking about your phone, and actively pay attention to the material to be learned, it can make a difference (Whittington, 2019).

———•———

Study Tip 4.1: Check your environment to minimize extraneous load before you start to study. Put your phone away when studying.

———•———

Germane Load

Germane load refers to the cognitive energy devoted to processing and handling information. This one can have hugely impact learning. There are two important aspects of germane load: automaticity and schema activation.

Automaticity

Your brain is very good at putting more energy toward and getting more efficient at the activities you do frequently (Schneider & Chein, 2003). This is where that autopilot I mentioned at the beginning of the chapter comes from. There is huge benefit to an action or information being automatic. With no real cognitive expenditure necessary, an automatic task can be combined with another task. That is why you can simultaneously walk (automatic) and talk (not automatic; you have to think while doing it).

If you identify foundational terms, concepts, and processes in your academic work and practice them repeatedly to make them automatic, you will reduce cognitive load. With foundational tasks automatic, you can then put cognitive energy toward complex work. Here is a simple example: As a child, you probably had to learn sight words, such as "the," "and," "this," "mom," and "dad." You practiced these words over and over. Eventually, as soon as you saw the letter formation "a-n-d," you just knew the word was "and." You didn't have to think about it; it was automatic. Taken a step further, after the word "car" becomes automatic, as soon as you see the word, your brain pulls up "a small transportation device that is typically privately owned and holds one to five people," in about 0.25 seconds with no almost no cognitive load expended. That is the power of repetition. For your coursework, identify the foundational material and make it automatic. This is how students ace exams and how faculty members become experts in their field.

This is an important area to think seriously about generative artificial intelligence (GenAI), such as ChatGPT. GenAI can be beneficial and it can also be disastrous, depending on how you use it. Using GenAI to create quizzes and to check your work, can be extremely helpful for learning new material and practicing it to the level of automaticity (Bowen & Watson, 2024). However, if you don't learn foundational concepts or terms and let GenAI do that initial, heavy lift for you, it will feel easier, but it will actually keep you from learning. The problem is that if you don't have foundational material at an automatic level, then you don't have the cognitive capacity to later process more complex material. As an example, suppose a person learning to read decided they didn't need to learn thousands of different words and instead decided that they would just look up words as needed. Imagine if you had to look up every word in this sentence. Could you really understand what the material was about? And it would take you forever to read a page. Use GenAI to help you to learn—the same as you would any study aid—but put the work in to make sure you have a foundation of material. Some say they don't need the basics; they can look that up and will instead focus on critical thinking. But based on how we have seen learning works, if you don't know foundational material, what would you think critically about?

Schema Activation

As you interact with the world around you, your brain will naturally group similar information together. The grouping of information and understanding of how the pieces of information interact with one another is called a *schema*. Once schemas are in place, it is incredible how fast you can learn new things. We can use McDonald's as an example of a multiple schemas you already have. When you visit any McDonald's in the country, you know almost everything on their menu, how to order, and even where the restroom is likely to be. McDonald's is not known for the quality of their food; they are known for being fast. They have, on purpose, helped you to create a schema that reduces cognitive load so you don't end up standing at the counter asking a lot of questions. Similarly, when you walk into any classroom, you can use your knowledge of how classrooms are generally set up to figure out where you'll sit and where the lecturer will stand. By pulling up the "classroom schema," your brain now only needs to secure a few pieces of vital information, such as the front of the room, so you know where to sit.

As you learn new material, think of already-known information about that material (that's your existing schema). The new information becomes much easier to learn, because you just need to tuck it into your existing schema. An added advantage is that you then create increasingly complex schemas. This is another part of how individuals become experts.

Key Factors to Deep Learning

Learning is incredibly nuanced, and due to the length of this book, I am able only to present a few foundational concepts. The good news is that some universal elements must always exist, or learning is very challenging, if not impossible. This is true whether you are learning to tie your shoes or about the Krebs cycle in biology or how to multiply fractions. If you are mindful of the following universal principles, you can improve how you learn.

Attention

Take a minute right now, close your eyes, and listen carefully. What do you hear, smell, or physically feel now that you didn't notice before? A lot of stimuli (i.e., sights, sounds, smells, and body sensations from touching) reach your body, but not all are processed. Attention is the process of attending to a stimulus. If you don't attend to something, it is as if it never happened (e.g., a professor gives an example while you are texting a friend; you don't hear the example, and you don't recognize it when it shows up on the test).

Attention is the first step in the learning process (Lindsay, 2020). If you don't attend to a stimulus, there is no way for you to learn anything about or from that stimulus. In class, it is important to force yourself to attend to what is happening. If your professor is lecturing, listen. You may be tempted to check out something on your laptop or think about what you will do over the weekend. When you do so, your attention moves away from the material being presented, and you no longer attend to the lecture information. Look for ways to improve attention, like coming up with possible test questions during class as the material is being presented. If you are in a small group, listen to what is being said; do not focus on what your response will be. When you are reading, check periodically to be sure your focus is on the material you are reading. It is common for your mind to wander as you read. By completing periodic self-checks of your attention, you will catch when you need to regain focus and return your mind to reading. It is challenging but do your best to practice focusing your attention. That will at least start the learning process.

Value

The next critical part of learning is finding some value in the information. You might be aware of two people talking at the table next to you, but you may not care about what they are talking about until one of the two people says the name of your best friend. The value of the conversation suddenly increases. At this point, you are not only going to pay more attention to the conversation, you are much more likely to remember what was said.

As you attend lectures, work in small groups, and read assigned material, keep looking for value. If you think to yourself, "I don't know why I have to read this stuff. I am never going to have any use for it in my life," you are signalling to your brain that the information is not worth spending the time to process the information in a way that will make it available later. Why would your brain spend the germane load to build a schema if you don't expect to see it again? Try to make the information relevant to you. For example, a lecture on the inner ear, which controls balance, could conjure up visions of yourself balancing during basketball practice. If you can find ways to bring value to what you are learning, it will be easier to learn and also easier to remember later.

Understanding

Along with attention and value, the new information must be understandable. If you don't understand what is being presented, your brain won't know what to do with the new information, because it won't know which schema to activate. This explains the feeling you get when a person is telling a story or explaining a concept that you just don't "get," even though you were paying close attention. If you realize you lost focus, you might say, "Wait, what happened after he walked into the restaurant?" or "Could you please explain again how molecules move from a trans to a cis configuration?"

Study Tip 4.2: One of the best ways to learn is to teach the new thing to someone else. If a person is not available, teach it to ChatGPT or some other GenAI program. Tell the GenAI program you want to role-play you as the teacher and GenAI as the student. Then ask the GenAI program to give you feedback on how well you explained the concept.

Anticipation of Success

The final important universal component of learning for this section is a belief that you will be able to learn the material. Yes, this is self-efficacy, the same concept introduced in Chapter 2. Just as a sports team that feels it cannot win often loses, if you think you can't learn something (low self-efficacy), it is unlikely you will learn it. Part of the reason is cognitive load. If you are thinking to yourself "I can't learn this. I will never get it," these thoughts become extraneous load that max out your cognitive load. It is fine to recognize material is challenging, but with all the resources pointed out in this book, you can learn just about anything. It won't be easy, but you can do it. When you believe that and focus on learning, your probability of learning increases dramatically.

Chapter Summary

Learning is a natural process that we all do every day, but few think about the process. Learning in classrooms follows the same basic principles as all learning. All learning is limited by cognitive load, specifically intrinsic and extrinsic load. Germane load, comprised of automaticity and schemas, will take a bit of work up front, but in the long run, these can greatly enhance learning. The components of intrinsic, extraneous, and germane load work together to indicate the amount of information that can be processed at any given time.

When it comes to learning, a few universal components need to be present for any learning, whether in a college course, working at a job, or teaching children to pick up toys. These elements are attention, value, understanding, and anticipation of success.

Discussion Questions

1 Think about a place you like to study and list five sources of *extraneous* load in that space. How might you reduce these?
2 Think about the last time you studied or did homework for any class. How would you rate the material in that study session on a scale of 1 (very low *intrinsic* load) to 10 (very high *intrinsic* load)? How did you arrive at your rating of the material?
3 Describe one thing outside of college and academics for which you have a schema. How does having that schema help you to learn something new that is related to that schema? It can be from shopping, sports, going to a friend's house, or any other aspect of your life.
4 Explain something that you learned recently using the concepts of attention, value, understanding, and anticipation of success.

References

Azevedo, F. A., Carvalho, L. R., Grinberg, L. T., Farfel, J. M., Ferretti, R. E., Leite, R. E., Filho, W. J., Lent, R., & Herculano-Houzel, S. (2009). Equal numbers of neuronal and nonneuronal cells make the human brain an isometrically scaled-up primate brain. *Journal of Comparative Neurology*, *513*(5), 532–541. https://doi.org/10.1002/cne.21974

Bowen, J. A., & Watson, C. E. (2024). *Teaching with AI: A practical guide to a new era of human learning*. John Hopkins Press.

Kumaradevan, K. S., Balan, A., Khan, K., Alji, R. M., & Narayanan, S. N. (2021). Modulatory role of background music on cognitive interference task in young people. *Irish Journal of Medical Science*, *190*, 779–786. https://doi.org/10.1007/s11845-020-02365-6

Lindsay, G. W. (2020). Attention in psychology, neuroscience, and machine learning. *Frontiers in Computational Neuroscience*, *14*(29). https://doi.org/10.3389/fncom.2020.00029

Schneider, W., & Chein, J. M. (2003). Controlled & automatic processing: Behavior, theory, and biological mechanisms. *Cognitive Science*, *27*(3), 525–559. https://doi.org/10.1016/S0364-0213(03)00011-9

Sweller, J. (1988). Cognitive load during problem solving: Effects on learning. *Cognitive Science*, *12*(2), 257–285. https://doi.org/10.1207/s15516709cog1202_4

Whittington, B. L. (2019). Benefits of a voluntary cell phone abstinence intervention in general psychology courses. *Teaching of Psychology*, *46*(4), 299–305. https://doi.org/10.1177/0098628319872575

5

ENHANCING YOUR MEMORY

Learning and memory work together, but they are different processes. Learning is the acquisition of new information. *Memory is the record of learning that can be produced when needed.* Sometimes you think you remember something, but find out later you are unable to produce the information or process you need during an exam or when called on in class. That happened to me several times as an undergraduate until I realized I needed to *practice* at recall to determine if I *could* recall the information that I needed when I needed it. After I realized the importance of practice, my grades improved quickly.

Forming memories is not new to you; you remember things all the time. Just like you are learning all the time. How you remember everyday things is very similar to how you remember academic things, and you can improve your memory with practice.

Memory Processes

There are three primary cognitive processes involved in remembering new information and making that memory last: encoding, consolidation, and retrieval (Melton, 1963).

Encoding

The items or processes we store for later use are usually not exact replicas of what we experience. The information we wish to retain is first encoded. *Encoding* is how the brain takes information from the world and creates a memory trace. There are different types of encoding that allow us to process different

DOI: 10.4324/9781003499176-7

types of information. We have encoding for each of our senses, which is how we can have memories associated with smells (grandmother's oatmeal cookies) and sounds (our dog barking). Of the senses, vision is most often used, and through *visual encoding*, we take images we see and convert them into memory traces. Some memory trace images can persist for our entire life, like images of a house you grew up in, a first kiss, or the day you arrived at college.

Semantic encoding lets us process the concepts we hear, stories we read in a book, or scenes we watch in a movie and turns the information into memory traces that have a precise meaning or information that can be used in a specific context. Much of the content you learn in class is coded semantically.

These encoding processes mean that you are constantly converting information from your encounters into pieces of information that you can store as different kinds of memory traces. Typically, initial memory traces are weak and can be lost easily if some other inputs disrupt it. *Disruption*, also called interference, inhibits your recall of the new weak information. This process of interference is a serious problem for classroom learning. On any given day, if you have a political science course and right after that class you have intro to sociology, the information you learn in sociology will interfere with the learning in the political science course. You can still learn, but it will be more challenging to remember information later. This is why it is helpful to avoid back-to-back classes if possible, and block off 30 minutes to review the material, or rewrite your notes, soon after class before the memory trace is disrupted. If you practice going over new material, you can strengthen the memory trace. The faster after learning you practice, the more likely you are to create a strong memory that is not disrupted by other information.

Study Tip 5.1: Review key material you learned shortly after class or completing homework, then once every few days after that to strengthen your memory of that information.

Consolidation

The second memory process is *consolidation*, which helps stabilize the new memory as it is strengthened and integrated into preexisting knowledge, often in the form of a schema. The more you already know about a topic, the better schemas you have for that information, or the more you repeat the information, the stronger the consolidation of the memory trace and the more stable the memory. Maybe you meet Jada at a party. Your best friend has already told several fun stories about Jada, so it's easy to add her name to an existing schema at the time you see her. Or maybe you have never heard about her, but you purposefully user her name several times during the conversation, so it sticks. The same process is true with new information you learn in any course. One of the best things you can do any time you learn something new is to put it to use right away. If you learn a new word, try to use it several times in the hours after learning the word. If you learn about a new system in biology, think about similar systems. If you do something with the new material several times, ideally soon after encountering it, the memory trace will keep getting stronger and the likelihood that you will remember it later increases.

Retrieval

The final memory process is retrieval. *Retrieval* is the process of accessing the memory trace of the item you are interested in and then making it available to you for use. Retrieval is closely tied to consolidation; when you retrieve information, you process the information again and repeat connections that also help consolidate the information all over again. You may be pairing the old information with new information and reinserting the information into the same knowledge network or, if the information has changed, into a new knowledge network. This process is called reconsolidation, and every time it happens, the memory gets stronger (Nader & Hardt, 2009). You never know what information you will need down the road, so it is best to have as many pieces of information, schemas, and connections among information and schemas as you can.

Memory Enhancements

Earlier I mentioned that you are constantly learning and remembering information. Nobody needs to teach you *how* to remember. However, I suspect you will find *strengthening* your memory valuable. Researchers have been studying human memory for over 100 years, with early work on Ebbinghaus's (1913) forgetting curve, which is still being actively researched today (DeSoto & Roediger, 2019). The forgetting curve shows that we forget material at an exponential rate; we forget a lot quickly, then the loss slows over time. As an example, if you learn something in your biology, math, history, or language course, unless you work to encode, consolidate, and retrieve it, most people will forget about half of what they learned in a day or two, and 90% of the new information is gone in about a month. In other words, if your first exam is in early October, if you don't practice and rehearse what you have learned, about 90% of what you learned will be gone by Thanksgiving. By the comprehensive final in December, if there is material you have not thought about or used since the first part of the semester, you won't be reviewing the material—it will be necessary to learn much of the information all over again.

I learned this the hard way in Calculus 1. The course started okay—there were four exams, one final, and optional homework assignments. I didn't do any of the assignments—in hindsight, poor idea number one—and I stayed up all night before each exam to learn that exam's information—poor idea number two. After bombing the first test, I earned high Bs and low As on the rest of the unit exams. The problem is that although I did well on unit exams, I did not restudy or reuse the material across time, and no consolidation from sleep missed by cramming meant I forgot most of the information within a few days. About a week before the final, I started to review the course information to study for the final, and I quickly realized I was in trouble. Nearly everything I had learned the first half of the semester and much of the second half was gone. I studied the best I could for the final, but there was too much to relearn. I scored a 37% (by far the lowest exam score I had ever received).

I have seen this pattern repeatedly among my students. It even happened to a few students in my junior-level Learning and Memory course. That hurt a bit, because we talked about the concept in class. If you pass or even do well on unit exams and flunk the final, it is likely not because the final exam was particularly difficult. The poor final exam score is because of how you learned and then used (or failed to use) the material learned. Following are four ways you can keep from losing the information you worked so hard to learn. There are more, but these are the most researched right now.

Elaboration

The word *elaboration* means to add detail. For memory elaboration, the idea is to create alternative paths to a memory trace (Bartsch & Oberauer, 2020). The more you can connect the information to what you already know (your preexisting schemas), the more quickly you can access and understand that new information. For example, if you just learned about sedimentary rocks in a geology course, you might think about how the rocks would form a layer cake. This would allow you to use your schema for cakes to help add detail to what you are learning about layers of rocks.

Elaboration strategies lighten your cognitive load. Anything that puts information into your own words is a good form of elaboration. One easy method is augmented notes. Take notes in class in a standard way, then, within 12 hours, go over the notes and rewrite concepts in your own words. If appropriate, come up with an example for concepts or terms.

Repetition

Each time a memory trace is activated, the memory strengthens. If you remember this from the germane cognitive load section in Chapter 4, congratulations, you just strengthened that memory trace! The brain perceives information or tasks that are recalled or performed many times as important, and the recall or task becomes easier and easier. Maybe on the first day of the biology lab, you had a hard time operating the microscope, or perhaps you had a hard time recalling the quadratic equation in algebra, but after using the microscope for each lab and working out some quadratic equations, things improved. It is obvious, but important to point out, that the task did not get easier. *The more you did it, the lower the cognitive load, and the better you got.* In psychology studies, we call this effect of repetition "the testing effect." When you take tests, you read a question and pull up an answer. The more tests you take, the better you become at pulling up answers. This is why some of your teachers give a lot of quizzes. They are trying to help you strengthen memory traces.

It is also important to point out that you may know people who learn the material very quickly and seemingly with less effort than you. They may have a stronger background in the area or have already practiced the types of problems you are solving. The point is that everyone must put in the energy to learn. Some do it well before the class and others in the class, but everyone must work to learn at some point. They aren't necessarily a better learner.

A team of researchers in Sweden who specialize in studying how the brain functions found that the testing effect works for students at all cognitive levels (Jonsson et al., 2021). Regardless of how you are doing in class, you will very likely benefit from the testing effect. You can do this independently by making flash cards, answering questions at the end of the chapter, doing practice tests, and working with a friend to quiz each other. Generative artificial intelligence (GenAI), such as ChatGPT or CoPilot, can also be helpful for practicing re-calling new information to strengthen your memory of it. To accomplish this, research is showing a positive effect of using AI chatbots to improve student learning outcomes (Wu & Yu, 2023). Have GenAI quiz you over material in different ways until you can easily retrieve the new information. For example, if you just learned about sunk cost, ask GenAI to create five multiple-choice questions about sunk cost. You can also type out what you think sunk cost is and then ask a GenAI program to tell you if you are correct or ask GenAI to explain the concept you have typed in a more accurate way. Each iteration of practice is retrieving information and strengthening memory traces.

Remember, learning anything new is often challenging at first, but it will get easier with repetition. I have been teaching for many years and have seen the same situation repeatedly. The students who practice regularly always become stronger students in my classes, even if they struggle at first.

Study Tip 5.2: Request that a GenAI program ask you a short-answer question about a concept. Type your response, and then ask GenAI to tell you what grade you get for that response. Rewrite your answer, and ask it for a grade again. This repetition will help you learn and help teach you how to write a good short-answer response.

Interleaving

Interleaving is a bit like weaving material. Instead of learning new material in blocks, such as studying Chapter 1 and then studying Chapter 2, weave the material together, maybe by using terms from Chapter 1 as you define terms in Chapter 2 and come up with an application example that uses information from both Chapters 1 and 2. This is very different from how college has been taught and students have learned for a very long time. This approach is important because this is one situation in which the learning you do in a college classroom is very different from your learning in everyday life. As noted, college is typically taught and learned in blocks of material. Exams are even frequently constructed so that the order of the test questions matches the order of the material in the book. Learning in life is not like that at all. Instead of information being sequential like it is in your courses, material in life is interleaved, repeating and alternating with new information. Interleaving your course material will make a positive difference in your recall and understanding.

Researchers note that interleaving keeps material in your brain much longer, and even more so when the concepts are similar to one another (Brunmair & Richter, 2019). When students study material and are tested using an interleaving system, they tend to do much better on the final and remember more information in classes the following semester. This does not mean you are going to like this approach. Students at the University of South Florida looked at hypothetical math class course syllabi and were instructed to select the course they felt would be most effective (Hartwig et al., 2022). Students rated the courses with interleaving as the least desirable, but those in the interleaved courses did better on tests. I know it looks more challenging when you first study and practice quizzing using an interleaved approach, but it is much better for learning. It will help you remember information when you take final exams, in future courses, and after you graduate.

Spaced Recall Practice

As has already been noted in this chapter, retrieving information multiple times helps keep that information in memory longer. It is common in college for students to cram for exams the night before the test. Sure, you may be retrieving information several times throughout the night, but the retrievals happen too close together in time to be effective in helping you to remember the information later. By spacing out studying, you are spacing out when you practice recalling information, which means memory traces exist longer. Just about the time a memory may be ready to fade, you attend a practice session, and the memory trace is strengthened yet again.

Research agrees, spaced practice wins nearly every time. A group of psychologists from the University of California-San Diego conducted a meta-analysis (reviewed many studies) on cramming versus spacing out studying (Cepeda et al., 2006). Out of 271 studies, 259 showed better results for spacing out studying, and only 12 showed better or equivalent results for cramming. In one study, students took a test right after a cumulative review session (equivalent to a session of cramming), whereas other students had review sessions spread out over several weeks. Students who had been doing spaced reviews scored 9% higher on the actual test. When the material was tested a month later, students who had completed spaced out reviews scored 22% higher than those who only crammed. That's a bit more than a two-letter-grade difference! It is easy to fall into a cramming study method, but you will be a much stronger learner if you set up a schedule and regularly space out study sessions. It is also much less stressful the night before the exam.

Chapter Summary

Memory and learning are different concepts, and information regarding the fundamental process for remembering is presented in this chapter: encoding (taking in the information), consolidation (finding a place to store the memory), and retrieval (getting the desired information and making it known). Several evidence-based approaches to strengthening memory are presented in this chapter, including the processes of elaboration, repetition, interleaving, and spaced recall. The disadvantages of cramming are also explained, along with why studying over time results in better memories of material in the long run.

Discussion Questions

1 What is your current primary strategy to remember new material? Describe it using the concepts of encoding, consolidation, and retrieval. What new strategies could you develop to study for a test (e.g., reviewing notes 15–30 mins after class, creating quizzes for yourself, etc.)? Finally, for courses currently in your schedule, where could you go right after class to review notes for 15–30 minutes? Do you currently engage in that process?
2 Protecting a memory trace and strengthening it are important so as not to lose the newly learned information. Select one of the strategies noted at the end of the chapter—elaboration, repetition, interleaving, and spaced recall—and explain how you would use the technique to study material from this chapter.
3 What material in college do you struggle with the most? Using the concepts from this book, why do you think it is so hard to learn the material you are struggle with?

References

Bartsch, L. M., & Oberauer, K. (2020). The effects of elaboration on working memory and long-term memory across age. *Journal of Memory and Language, 118*, 1–16. https://doi.org/10.1016/j.jml.2020.104215

Brunmair, M., & Richter, T. (2019). Similarity matters: A meta-analysis of interleaved learning and its moderators. *Psychological Bulletin, 145*(11), 1029–1052. https://doi.org/10.1037/bul0000209

Cepeda, N. J., Pashler, H., Vul, E., Wixted, J. T., & Rohrer, D. (2006). Distributed practice in verbal recall tasks: A review and quantitative synthesis. *Psychological Bulletin, 132*(3), 354–380. https://doi.org/10.1037/0033-2909.132.3.354

DeSoto, K. A., & Roediger, H. L., III. (2019). Remembering the presidents. *Current Directions in Psychological Science, 28*(2), 138–144. https://doi.org/10.1177/0963721418815685

Ebbinghaus, H. (1913). *Memory: A contribution to experimental psychology* (H. Ruger & C. Bussenius, Trans.). Teachers College Press. https://doi.org/10.1037/10011-000

Hartwig, M. K., Rohrer, D., & Dedrick, R. F. (2022). Scheduling math practice: Students' underappreciation of spacing and interleaving. *Journal of Experimental Psychology: Applied*. Advance online publication. https://doi.org/10.1037/xap0000391

Jonsson, B., Wiklund-Hörnqvist, C., Stenlund, T., Andersson, M., & Nyberg, L. (2021). A learning method for all: The testing effect is independent of cognitive ability. *Journal of Educational Psychology, 113*(5), 972–985. https://doi.org/10.1037/edu0000627

Melton, A. W. (1963). Implications of short-term memory for a general theory of memory. *Journal of Verbal Learning and Verbal Behavior, 2*(1), 1–21. https://doi.org/10.1016/S0022-5371(63)80063-8

Nader, K., & Hardt, O. (2009). A single standard for memory: The case for reconsolidation. *Nature Reviews Neuroscience, 10*(3), 224–234. https://doi.org/10.1038/nrn2590

Wu, R., & Yu, Z. (2023). Do AI chatbots improve student learning outcomes? Evidence from a meta-analysis. *British Journal of Educational Technology, 55*(1), 10–33. https://doi.org/10.1111/bjet.13334

6

EXPLORING SOCIAL INFLUENCES

Learning and memory are rooted in cognitive psychology, the study of how humans process information. Another area of psychology that is important, yet often left out when we talk about how people learn, is social psychology. Social psychologists study how a person's thoughts, feelings, and behaviors affect themselves and other people (Kasin et al., 2021). Much of this chapter includes topics that emerge when individuals combine cognitive psychology and social psychology to form a specialty area of social cognition. Understanding a bit about social cognition is critical for learning in harmony with your brain, because our brains are wired for both thinking and social interaction (Schmidt et al., 2021).

There are many important concepts within the area of social cognition. For this chapter I have selected three that are extremely important in college: *mindset*, *metacognition*, and *attribution*. These three concepts worked together to make the first 2 months of college almost my last. I was shocked when I received an F minus minus on a test (*lack of metacognition*) and believed my failures were *attributed* to me not being smart (*a fixed mindset*). Had I possessed the information in this chapter, I could have made positive adjustments much more quickly.

Mindset

Carol Dweck (2007), a psychologist at Stanford University, developed the concept of mindset, noting that individuals have either a fixed mindset or a growth mindset in different aspects of their lives. A fixed-minded person believes they were born with a fairly set level of intelligence, certain talents, and abilities. When a person has this belief, practice and effort in an area might help a bit, but

DOI: 10.4324/9781003499176-8

they generally believe that you either "have it" or you don't. Growth-minded people, on the other hand, believe that intelligence, talents, and abilities change throughout a person's life depending on the extent to which the individual works to improve. Once you recognize when you are falling into a fixed-mindset trap, you have the opportunity to create new opportunities for learning.

The Origins of Fixed-Mindedness

Fixed-mindedness makes it challenging to become better. Unfortunately, it doesn't take much for a person to become fixed-minded. Mueller and Dweck (1998) found that a person can be impacted after just one exposure. For example, a teacher may say to a child, "Another 100%. You are so smart," or "Scoring two goals in a soccer game is amazing. You are a natural." Those messages convey to the child that they have a gift or a natural ability. The child assumes that intelligence and talent are inherent characteristics, and they are happy to have them. Such a child develops a fixed mindset of being smart or being talented. Sadly, the opposite is also true: If teachers tell students that they are "dumb" or "naturally clumsy," the students develop a negative fixed mindset, seeing themselves as lacking intelligence or talent.

This can happen for writing, math, speaking, drawing, playing sports, and nearly anything that you might do. I developed a fixed mindset regarding writing in middle school, when a teacher told me that some people are good writers and others are not—and I was in the "not good" group. All through high school and college I received grades of C and below on papers. I never tried to get better, because I "knew" I was not "a good writer." Now I realize that my writing never improved because I didn't think I *could* improve my writing, making my bad grades on papers a self-fulfilling prophecy. If there is any area in which you flat out say, "I am not good at (fill in the blank)," you, like me, developed a fixed mindset at some point in your life.

People often ask, "If you can't say a person is smart, or a natural, how can you praise them?" The answer is simply to focus on the effort put into a task. For example, it is entirely appropriate to say, "A 100%! You must have studied hard for this one." Or "Great game today, I can tell you have been doing your drills!" The praises here signal that working at something pays off and, ostensibly, working harder means they grow by getting better. This cultivates a growth mindset.

Spotting a Fixed Mindset

There are several ways to spot a fixed-minded person. One easy sign is that fixed-minded people do not take criticism well or use bad grades as a motivation to work harder for the next assignment or test. Criticism is seen as personal, and they will overreact, tell you that your assessment of them not being successful was flawed, or offer justification as to why there was no way they could complete the outcome at the expected level. While returning tests, I periodically hear students in class say quietly to their neighbors, "That test was ridiculous. He is so unreasonable. There is no way anyone could pass that test." On most such occasions, the average in class was around a B –. A person with a fixed mindset may also quit something or not even start if there is the slightest chance that they will fail. If you are playing a game of ping-pong against a fixed-minded person, and you score the first five points, your opponent may well find a very good reason to quit. Fixed-minded people avoid the risk of finding out (or being found out) that they are not excellent at something.

Mindsets Are Context Specific

Individuals don't have an overall fixed or growth mindset for all things. They develop mindsets for each behavior or skill set. Several years ago, I had a student, who I'll call Sam, in my statistics class. Sam explained to me that they "couldn't do math" (classic fixed mindset). We talked for a bit until Sam had to leave for basketball practice, looking forward to the practice even though it was exhausting and challenging. Sam had improved a lot that year in basketball, because the coach had the team practicing fundamentals and drills. Sam didn't improve in math because they felt it was a waste of time to work at something "impossible" to improve. Sam had a growth mindset for basketball and a fixed mindset for math at the same time.

Becoming Growth-Minded

You can shift to being more growth-minded. First, change your self-talk. Instead of saying to yourself, "I can't," shift to saying, "I can't *yet*." Second, try to work just a little, on something small, in an area you have always felt you "couldn't do." As soon as you are successful on the small task, set a goal for something else a bit bigger. This is how growth works. It can be frustrating if you are way behind others, but they also had to start small at first. The idea is to change your mindset to see that you can work and get better at just about anything. Remember that I mentioned earlier how I struggled with writing. After becoming a college teacher, I turned down writing opportunities, because I had a negative fixed mindset about my writing. I saw myself as someone who couldn't write. Susan, an editor at a college textbook publishing house, finally convinced me to write one short chapter. When I submitted that chapter, she told me it was one of the best she had seen in years. My immediate response was, "That's not possible; I'm not good at writing." About a year later, I finished that book, and thanks to that success, I started to see writing from a growth-minded perspective. Since that first book, I have published many articles and individual chapters. The book in your hands would never have happened without someone convincing me to try. Unfortunately, for many years I didn't think I could write, and because I didn't know a person could get better at writing by practicing, I didn't even try.

Third, in your head, change "failure" to "feedback." Getting something wrong is a great part of learning. If you always get everything right, then you are not testing your abilities. Feedback is a game plan for getting better. Perhaps the best message to keep at heart is a quote attributed to Nelson Mandela, "I never lose. I either win or I learn" (Pelzer, 2020, para. 3).

It is important to note that although you can *always* improve, as they say, "results may vary." Your classmates have different backgrounds—maybe your roommate took AP Biology in high school, but your school didn't offer AP classes. If you are both in Biology 101, your roommate might study for 1 hour and get an A, whereas your 10 hours earns a B+. Don't see that as being unfair. You may have to study more hours than your roommate because they already put in that study time in high school. But as you move to more advanced biology classes, you will get closer to the same skill level. You may well surpass your roommate! In my many years teaching many students, I have often seen a "superstar" in class passed by individuals who outworked them throughout the semester. The practice paid off.

––––––●––––––

Study Tip 6.1: Be growth-minded, seek out feedback whenever you can, and listen carefully to the feedback given.

––––––●––––––

Metacognition

Metacognition is generally defined as the process of thinking about one's thinking in relation to self (Dennis & Sommerville, 2023). When you think about why you did a particular thing, or to what extent you are good at something, you are engaging in the process of metacognition. For example, you may have engaged in metacognition during a test when you thought to yourself, "Okay, I know this one. I remember how excited I was when I 'got it' during my study session last Tuesday." Unfortunately, people rarely engage in metacognitive thinking in any kind of systematic way. This is because we do many things with our brain on autopilot, made possible by automaticity. The autopilot function works well in many situations, but being aware of what is happening allows you to make corrections so you can improve. If you practice metacognitive strategies, you will become a much stronger learner and, unlike me, never be in a position of being surprised if you flunk a chemistry test.

Understanding Metacognition

Metacognition is one of the most studied areas in psychology because it helps us to move from cognitively passive learners to cognitively active learners (Stanger-Hall, 2012). Think about how you prepare for an exam. Looking over notes or reading the textbook without a plan are cognitively passive strategies and what most students do. You are cognitively active in your exam preparation when you think about what specific areas you need to study and for how long, when you turn headings of class notes into questions, and when you think about how you'll approach answering questions on the test.

This is critical, because if learners are not cognitively active in their processing, they tend to make the same errors over and over. As an example, a student (let's call them Jules) told me they had started statistics three times but dropped the class each time after failing the first exam. Jules said flat out that they were just "bad at math and couldn't pass this required course." If this sounds to you like a story that belongs in the mindset material, you are understanding this material, as Jules obviously had a fixed mindset. I tell this story here because I helped Jules become a metacognitive learner.

To get started with metacognition, I talked to Jules about what they were thinking regarding the material. As part of their awareness of their thoughts, Jules was to try and frame things in terms of "I can't *yet*" (implying the possibility for growth) and avoid negative thoughts like "Statistics is stupid" (as your brain tends not to retain what you tell it has no value). This is a solid example of active metacognitive thinking and consistent with researchers who found that metacognition is most effective when it is used specifically to make changes in a focused learning context (Zohar & David, 2009). I will let you know what happened to Jules in a bit.

Metacognitive Regulation

Metacognition is thinking about thinking, but *metacognitive regulation* is the way in which you direct your thinking. Three important skills when it comes to metacognitive regulation are planning, monitoring, and evaluating (Tanner, 2012). First is *planning*; don't just grab a book and head to the library. Use metacognitive strategies to set yourself up for success. Start by thinking about what is expected for this assignment or exam. What resources are preferred, and which are most valuable? What food can I prepare ahead of time for lunch or for a snack, so I don't have to stop working and go looking for food? Where will I study, for how long, and how? Who should I study with, or should I study alone? Plan what you need; it's an important life principle.

The second skill is *monitoring* while you are studying. Jules did this by directing their thoughts away from the negative/self-limiting ones. Researchers at Hofstra University looked at student success in moving from high school to college (Santangelo et al., 2021). In high school, one can get by using surface reading techniques, but metacognitive monitoring techniques are important in college, because the material is more challenging. Santangelo and colleagues found that, three semesters into college, the students who engaged in metacognitive monitoring were much more likely to have persisted or graduated (81.4%) than those who did not (55%). One way to monitor while reading (or other studying) is to do a quick mental check-in after each section, every few pages, or every 15 minutes or so. All you need to do is pause, look away from the book, and explain to yourself the major concept just read. I have ADHD, so I often need to do this every 5–10 minutes while reading journal articles and books. If your mind is wandering, using this strategy allows you to catch it quickly and keep from wasting time.

The third metacognitive *regulation* skill is evaluating. This skill refers to you reflecting on the effectiveness of a strategy used to write a paper, study for an exam, or take the exam. Is the level to which you know the material appropriate given the time and energy spent studying? If not, then some adjustment is necessary. This skill of evaluating also helps you use information from past events to predict future events. For example, if you grossly underestimate how much time it will take to write a paper, you may end up writing for 12 hours straight the night before a term paper is due. When it comes to studying, one effective technique to do this is called the muddiest point (Angelo & Zakrajsek, 2024). At the end of study or class session, write down what you understand least. Then, the next time you study, start by looking that up and filling that learning gap.

Jules, the student struggling in my stats class, used metacognitive evaluation by predicting how they would perform before starting the exam and how they felt after answering the last question. These forms of evaluation are sometimes called metacognitive checks. As your skill improves, the grade you estimate at the start of the exam should be more and more similar to the grade you estimate after taking the exam. Keep a log of before-the-exam and after-the-exam estimates in a notebook or on your phone so you can track your progress. The goal is to get close estimates *and* evaluate how well your metacognitive strategies are working. You'll be able to determine how much study time you need and also be able to see at a glance if your study strategies are still effective.

Jules ended up with a C in my class and was as happy as anyone who's taken any of my classes. As statistics was required in the psychology department, the C in that class let Jules stay in the program. Two years later, Jules told me at graduation that the metacognitive strategies learned in statistics were also very helpful in other classes. Not all these strategies will work for everyone all the time, but if you *do* work at it, you will continue to improve at learning.

———————•◆•———————

Study Tip 6.2: When using metacognitive evaluation, don't forget to note when you accurately predict how well you know something.

———————•◆•———————

Attribution

In 1958, Fritz Heider, a social psychologist at the University of Kansas, researched how people decided *why* people do things (Heider, 1958). Imagine that you see a middle-aged man on the subway give up his seat to an elderly person who is having trouble standing. You might attribute his gesture to being kind. But suppose you then notice a police officer near that seat and a sign you didn't see before: "These seats reserved for the elderly. Improper use will result in a $200 fine." Given this new information, you might revise your attribution and conclude that rather than being kind, he gave up the seat to avoid a penalty.

Intrinsic Versus Extrinsic

According to attribution theory, we tend to make attributions that are external (about the environment) or internal (about the person). Internal attributions are also sometimes called *dispositional*, because they are based on the person's disposition. External attributions are also called *situational*, because it is inferred that something in the environment was the real cause for the behavior. In the example on the subway, when the person first gave up the seat, you may have given his behavior an internal/dispositional attribution (he's nice). However, once you saw the sign and the police officer, your attribution of his behavior may have switched to external/situational (he didn't want to get a ticket).

A Bit of Order, Please .

The overall goal of attribution theory is to make sense of the world (Kelley, 1967). If you are 5 minutes late to my office hours, I could attribute your lateness to an external cause, such as finding a parking spot, or to an internal cause, such as absentmindedness. My attribution is based on my social perception (that I like you) and is used to resolve the issue of your tardiness (must have been a problem parking). If a student of mine was lashing out in class, I might attribute their response to anger issues (internal). However, it would be different if they said that for the third day in a row, the cafeteria ran out of gluten-free options at breakfast, and they were hangry (external). Attribution helps us make sense of the world.

Fundamental Attribution Error

One important note on general rules for attribution is the fundamental attribution error (Ross, 1977). It is called *fundamental* because it happens a lot of the time. This attribution error is that we tend to think of other people's behavior as internal/dispositional and our own behavior as primarily external/situational.

The fundamental attribution error has many implications in our society. Flick and Schweitzer (2021), professors at the University of Wyoming, conducted a study about blame for traffic accidents. In mock trials, when a participant in the study was to assume that they themselves caused an accident, the participant saw the accident as due to poor visibility or bad windshield wipers (both external attributions). When a participant in the study was to assume that the other driver caused the accident, the participants said the other driver was being careless (internal attribution). This is a classic fundamental attribution error. Similarly, if you see a person with food insecurity using the food bank, you may immediately think the person is lazy and needs to get a job (internal). However, what if the person lost their job due to budget cuts (external) and nobody will hire them (external) in a recession? If we see others as more likely to be personally responsible for a negative outcome, due to the fundamental attribution error, it means our bias is having a negative effect.

Understanding attribution biases will have a significant impact on how you interact with others. If someone is being "rude," it might be that they are a jerk. Their behavior might also be due to an external cause. It's likely that whenever you are "rude" to someone, you allow yourself an external attribution (e.g., "I've been waiting longer! I'm tired, and my stomach hurts!"). It will also help with your own behaviors in many aspects of life, including making you a stronger learner. Each of us makes attributions about our behavior all the time, and, as with metacognition, if reflection and understanding are not actively used, we tend to make the same errors repeatedly.

Chapter Summary

Mindset is an explanatory model that identifies individuals' perceptions of behaviors. For a given area (e.g., math, giving presentations, taking tests), individuals tend to be either fixed- or growth-minded. Fixed-mindedness is generally the result of hearing and believing that ability is innate. Individuals with fixed mindsets tend not to take criticism well, have an inflated opinion of their abilities, and avoid risks. Overall, fixed-minded individuals see talent and intelligence as personality-defining and unchangeable concepts, whereas growth-minded individuals go through life looking for challenges and opportunities to gain skills, abilities, and knowledge. Individuals can learn to be more growth-minded.

Metacognition is knowing what you know or thinking about thinking. Metacognitive regulation allows learners to think about the material they are learning while learning it (plan, monitor, and evaluate). Attribution helps bring order to the world by determining why people do what they do. The primary attributions for behavior are internal (dispositional) and external (situational), and they depend on consistency and consensus. People tend toward fundamental attribution error, which is attributing behaviors of others to predominantly internal causes and our behavior to internal or external causes, depending on the situation.

Discussion Questions

1 Think of something you "can't do." What strategy could you use to shift that mindset? What would success look like if you could do the thing that you "can't do *yet*?"
2 Explain how you prepare for an exam, including where and how you study. Include any aspects of metacognition that you may already use. Explain one additional metacognitive strategy you could add.
3 Describe a situation in which a disagreement between two people may well have been the result of the fundamental attribution error. Include both what happened and how the fundamental attribution error contributed to the situation.

References

Angelo, T. A., & Zakrajsek, T. D. (2024). *Classroom assessment techniques: Formative feedback tools for college and university teachers*. Jossey-Bass.

Dennis, J. L., & Sommerville, M. P. (2023). Supportive thinking about thinking: Examining the metacognition theory-practice gap in higher education. *Higher Education, 86,* 99–117. https://doi.org/10.1007/s10734-022-00904-x

Dweck, C. S. (2007). *Mindset: The new psychology of success*. Ballantine Books.

Flick, C., & Schweitzer, K. (2021). Influence of the fundamental attribution error or perceptions of blame and negligence. *Experimental Psychology, 1*(4), 175–188. https://doi.org/10.1027/1618-3169/a000526

Heider, F. (1958). *The psychology of interpersonal relations*. Wiley. https://doi.org/10.1037/10628-000

Kasin, S., Fein, S., & Markus, H. R. (2021). *Social psychology* (11th ed.). Cengage.

Kelley, H. H. (1967). Attribution theory in social psychology. In D. Levine (Ed.), *Nebraska symposium on motivation* (Vol. 15, pp. 192–238). University of Nebraska Press.

Mueller, C. M., & Dweck, C. S. (1998). Praise for intelligence can undermine children's motivation and performance. *Journal of Personality and Social Psychology, 75*(1), 33–52. https://doi.org/10.1037//0022-3514.75.1.33

Pelzer, K. (2020). Get inspired to make an impact with these 75 famous Nelson Mandela quotes. *Parade.* https://parade.com/1074913/kelseypelzer/nelson-mandela-quotes/

Ross, L. (1977). The intuitive psychologist and his shortcomings: Distortions in the attribution process. In L. Berkowitz (Ed.), *Advances in experimental social psychology* (pp. 173–220). Academic Press. https://doi.org/10.1016/s0065-2601(08)60357-3

Santangelo, J., Cadieux, M., & Zapata, S. (2021). Developing student metacognitive skills using active learning with embedded metacognitive instruction. *Journal of STEM Education, 22*(2), 75–87. https://www.jstem.org/jstem/index.php/JSTEM/article/view/2475/2215

Schmidt, S. N. L., Hass, J., Kirsch, P., & Mier, D. (2021). The human mirror neuron system—A common neural basis for social cognition? *Psychophysiology, 58*(5), e13781. https://doi.org/10.1111/psyp.13781

Stanger-Hall, K. F. (2012). Multiple-choice exams: An obstacle for higher-level thinking in introductory science classes. *Cell Biology Education—Life Sciences Education, 11*(3), 294–306. https://doi.org/10.1187/cbe.11-11-0100

Tanner, K. D. (2012). Promoting student metacognition. *CBE—Life Sciences Education, 11*(2), 113–120. https://doi.org/10.1187/cbe.12-03-0033

Zohar, A., & David, A. B. (2009). Paving a clear path in a thick forest: A conceptual analysis of a metacognitive component. *Metacognition Learning, 4*(3), 177–195. https://doi.org/10.1007/s11409-009-9044-6

PART 3

Support Your Learning

7

FINDING AND USING PATTERNS

There are patterns in nearly everything you will ever learn; if you can find them, it will make the learning process much easier. Therapists recognize patterns in the way clients present information, doctors seek patterns in disease models, marketing experts find patterns in consumer behavior, and gardeners lay out plants in visually pleasing patterns. Professors identify patterns that allow them to process new information by quickly assimilating it into an existing framework or schema. There are many patterns in the learning process, but if no one points this out to you, you likely haven't even learned to look for them. Finding patterns often makes the difference between struggling to understand a concept and grasping it easily. Researchers at MIT have found that, with training, your working memory can be improved (Thompson et al., 2016). To do this, we, as learners, can look for patterns in information and practice putting items into chunks and integrating new material into existing schemas. Finding patterns can also help you remember what you read. As you become more skilled in finding patterns in your academic studies, you will find it much easier to learn new information.

Patterns in Content

Patterns allow us to use prior knowledge to lessen cognitive load and more easily integrate new information. Two of the primary ways that identifying patterns will help you to learn is through chunking and schemas.

DOI: 10.4324/9781003499176-10

Chunking

Because our brains cannot process an unlimited amount of information, we have a learning gatekeeping device in place, ensuring only the more important things in our lives are coded and stored. The system that processes information of value to us is our *working memory* (Baddeley & Hitch, 1974), so named because it is where work is done encoding and processing information. Unfortunately, it takes time and effort to do this coding work. So, even though the sensory system can scan an almost unlimited amount of information, our working memory can process only five to nine items at a time (Miller, 1994; Paas & Ayers, 2014). In the 1950s, experimental psychologists began looking at ways to increase working memory limits, because if you can widen that restrictive path, then you can process more information. George Miller (1956/1994), a cognitive psychologist working at Harvard, discovered a way to hack this memory gatekeeper.

Miller found that although the average person could hold just seven plus or minus two (or five to nine) pieces of information, complexity didn't seem to matter, only the number of items. Holding a string of seven unrelated digits, such as 3, 1, 2, 5, 4, 7, 6 in your memory is difficult. But rearranging them into the sequence 1, 2, 3, 4, 5, 6, 7 creates a meaningful cluster of information referred to as a chunk. Because the chunk of information comprised of numbers one through seven has been practiced so much, it is processed automatically. Recall from the discussion of cognitive load that if something is automatic, it takes very little mental energy. Therefore, a brain that finds this pattern would not count seven items, but rather only one chunk, labeled, "numbers up to 7." You now have room for six more chunks of information! One might ask, "If the chunks were very elaborate, wouldn't that let you process a lot more information?" The answer is "yes!" for those who know how to "chunk" efficiently, which you can both learn and get better at as you practice (Miller, 1956/1994).

Let's try another example to see how much of a difference it makes to chunk material by recognizing patterns. Read through the following set of letters one time. Do not study the list, just read through the letters slowly (about one letter per second) and then cover them and see how many you can recall.

A V M U L H

That was a set of six letters. A lot of people can do six, although there are several factors that can cause a person to struggle even with six, such as distractions (extraneous load), being tired, or even being dehydrated. Lindseth and colleagues (2013) at the University of North Dakota showed in a controlled experiment that pilots who had lower fluid intake had significant decreases in cognitive performance. You will learn better if you stay hydrated. Now let's try another set of letters. Same routine, read them slowly one at a time, cover them, and see how many you can remember.

IHFQAMUZFS

That should have been more challenging. If no pattern is noted and the letters are processed individually, we are past that range of five to nine items. What happens if (or when) you hit a spot and realized you were not going to be able to remember the list? The most common response for individuals, and it happens with my students all the time, is that when it becomes apparent that a list or topic can't be remembered, the individual just stops trying. So, that should have shown what it is like to max out on a task. Let's try another one: Same procedure as last time.

COGNITIVELOAD

This list of letters is 13 items long. My guess is that you didn't even need to read through the letters slowly. You likely glanced at this and could immediately cover the page and write out all 13 letters with no errors and minimal cognitive energy. That is the power of finding a pattern. If you were to be quizzed over the last two sets, you would spend much more time on the list of 10 that started with "I" than you would for this list of 13 letters that starts with "C." The "C" list is longer, but if you were quizzed a few days later, you would likely score better on that longer list. Okay, last one: Same process as the previous letter sets. Read the letters, cover the letters, and see how many you can remember.

IWILLACETHEQUIZOVERTHISMATERIAL

This set contains 31 items. It may take you a few seconds to be sure you have the words memorized, but I suspect that in much less time than 31 seconds (reading at the pace of one letter per second) you would be ready for a quiz over the letters. Finding patterns to chunk information efficiently means that in a shorter amount of time you can learn more. Wouldn't it be great if you could study less and learn more? It is possible. Look for ways to chunk the information where possible, and put information in schemas, like the grocery list example earlier or other known frameworks, like words or processes with which you are familiar. The more you work at these things, the better you will get at learning.

Study Tip 7.1: As you study, look for categories of information to see where you can form chunks of information.

Schemas

From the section on cognitive load, remember that schemas also help process information quickly. That is because the information in a schema is a type of pattern you have identified or created. For example, suppose you are going to the grocery store to buy nine items: eggs, hamburger, potato chips, orange juice, toilet paper, shampoo, toothpaste, bacon, and hamburger buns. Remembering nine individual items is challenging, but if you can call up appropriate schemas, you can chunk your list and make it much easier to remember. For this example, you could use three schemas that you know well: bathroom (toilet paper, shampoo, toothpaste), breakfast (eggs, bacon, orange juice), and picnic lunch (hamburger, hamburger buns, potato chips). If you read the list twice and then later recall the three schemas of bathroom, breakfast, and picnic lunch, those items will serve as cues and make it much easier to go to the store and get all the appropriate items. Schemas let you process much more material faster and with less effort. The same concept can be used almost any course.

Common Reading Patterns

You obviously know how to read, but do you know how to read academic material? Learning to find patterns in college material can make a huge difference in your learning. There is a great deal of research about reading and how we process text (Moje et al., 2020; Peng et al., 2018).

Pattern for Reading a Textbook

When you read a novel, you likely do not want to see the last few pages because you don't want to ruin the story by finding out about the ending. When you read a textbook, you want the story spoiled as quickly as possible, because as soon as you know what the chapter is about, you can start creating schemas and looking for patterns in the material. First, find the pages that were assigned or decide the number you wish to read (10 pages may be enough for one study session). Next, find the chapter or section summary. It could be at the end or the beginning of the chapter or section. Read the chapter summary. This will tell you quickly what this chapter or section is about.

Study Tip 7.2: Skim the material quickly before you read it for learning to activate prior knowledge you have in that area.

After reading the chapter summary, go back to the first page of what you are going to read. The first time through, read only chapter headings and subheadings. Don't just flip through them, look at them seriously. This will also help prime you for the material. *Now* it is time to read. Your brain has a sense of what is coming, so it shouldn't be surprised, meaning you can pull up schemas as needed. With a bit of practice, these steps will not take much time and set you up to read the material much more effectively.

Pattern for Reading a Journal Article

To get started, review the assignment from your instructor. Why was this article assigned? The purpose for reading will clue you in on if you need to know details or perhaps just the overall gist of the article. It is often best to start by looking at the headings. They are typically consistent from article to article. Look at each of the headings and think of them as questions. Then, as you read, your goal will be to answer the questions. For example, the section labeled "Conclusion" becomes, "What is the conclusion?" Do that for each section. I suggest reading the abstract, then the introduction, then the conclusion, and then discussion. After that, if you need to know how the study was conducted, read the methods and results. Methods and results are typically the most challenging parts and will be easier after you better understand what the article was all about.

Pattern for Reading a Novel

It's important to look for *themes*. There will be obvious themes, but the real value of the material will typically be *subthemes*. Be sure to watch for the standard literary elements, such as *narrative point of view, symbolism, characters, plot, imagery, foreshadowing*, and *setting*. In terms of patterns, also watch for *repetition*: That's always important. The repetition may be a journey, moods, seasons, or anything else. Keep in mind that with novels, authors often bury the meaning to make you curious or use metaphors to make the writing more poetic or more interesting. A good novel is never just a story.

Chapter Summary

Our brains make sense of the world by using patterns to help organize the massive amount of sensory information in our lives. The amount of information humans can process is limited by working memory or how sensory information of interest is coded and stored as a long-term memory. Working memory capacity is impacted by schemas, cognitive load, and chunking. Some patterns are seen nearly universally, and chunking is a great way to lean on existing patterns.

This includes patterns in how different course material is written, depending on whether it is a textbook, journal article, novel, or other. Whenever patterns can be found and maximized, learning has the potential to be faster and better.

Discussion Questions

1   What kind of patterns have you used to help you learn or remember items in any class, going back to your first year of high school? If you do not recall using any patterns, list three classes that likely had strong patterns and briefly explain those patterns.
2   Because of Miller's (1956/1994) work, it is frequently said that working memory holds 7±2 pieces of information. But information that can be related in some way can be gathered into and considered as one chunk. Given this, how much information do you think short-term memory can really hold? Explain your rationale.
3   Describe the process you typically use to read textbooks. Is that different from the process you use to read novels? Explain the difference. Describe how your strategy for reading could change after reading this chapter to increase the effectiveness of your reading.

References

Baddeley, A. D., & Hitch, G. (1974). Working memory. *Psychology of Learning and Motivation, 8*, 47–89. https://doi.org/10.1016/S0079-7421(08)60452-1

Lindseth, P. D., Lindseth, G. N., Petros, T. V., Jensen, W. C., & Caspers, J. (2013). Effects of hydration on cognitive function of pilots. *Military Medicine, 178*(7), 792–798. https://doi.org/10.7205/MILMED-D-13-00013

Miller, G. A. (1994). The magical number seven, plus or minus two: Some limits on our capacity for processing information. *Psychological Review, 101*(2), 243–352. https://doi.org/10.1037/0033-295X.101.2.343 (Original work published 1956).

Moje, E. B., Afflerback, P. P., Enciso, P., & Lesaux, N. K. (Eds.). (2020). *Handbook of reading research* (Vol. V). Routledge.

Paas, F., & Ayres, P. (2014). Cognitive load theory: A broader view on the role of memory in learning and education. *Educational Psychology Review, 26*(2), 191–195. https://doi.org/10.1007/s10648-014-9263-5

Peng, P., Barnes, M., Wang, C., Wang, W., Li, S., Swanson, H. L., Dardick, W., & Tao, S. (2018). A meta-analysis on the relation between reading and working memory. *Psychological Bulletin, 144*(1), 48–76. https://doi.org/10.1037/bul0000124

Thompson, T. W., Waskom, M. L., & Gabrieli, J. D. E. (2016). Intensive working memory training produces functional changes in large-scale frontoparietal networks. *Journal of Cognitive Neuroscience, 28*(4), 575–588. https://doi.org/10.1162/jocn_a_00916

8

THRIVING IN HIGHER EDUCATION

There are unexplained aspects of college that professors assume are handed down from generation to generation, such as expected student behaviors and campus resources. They are things rarely listed in the course catalog or syllabi or detailed in advisor meetings. It all works well, unless you don't happen to know about them. Medical schools have long referred to this as the *hidden curriculum*. It is very real and can have a significant impact on your success in college (Jackson, 1990; Kelly, 2009). As a first-generation college student, I had no idea about these hidden aspects of expected college behavior, the things it was just assumed I would know. Retrospectively, this is a primary reason I began the process of withdrawing from college in my first semester. I didn't know about the student success and tutoring centers. I didn't know it was possible to drop a class. It may be obvious to those who understand the system, but in high school you could not drop a class just because you were failing. I didn't know a lot of things about the college campus landscape. Several of the things I learned along the way are presented in this chapter. Understanding more about these rarely discussed educational elements will give you more options and resources, and hopefully provide a stronger foundation for you to thrive, not just get by, in college.

Individual Versus Group Study

A recurring decision to make for each course is whether to study by yourself or find a study group. Different strategies work better under different circumstances, but overall, study groups have many benefits: They reduce procrastination, provide an opportunity to ask questions, decrease stress, and foster diverse perspectives. Members also hold each other accountable. However, there are

DOI: 10.4324/9781003499176-11

times it is better to work alone. Working alone has several advantages: studying at your own pace, fewer distractions, control over the environment, and the ability to set your schedule. Studying alone is also very good for establishing a foundation of knowledge. Another option is to study in pairs. Researchers have found the best result with students working in pairs versus students working alone or in groups of three or four (Kim et al., 2020).

Study Tip 8.1: Study alone, practice in pairs, and review in a group.

Determining the best way for you to study is crucial to your academic success. Try different approaches, and note which method works best under what circumstance using metacognitive strategies. For example, you could set up a group of four and then study in three "phases." First, each group member studies alone to learn foundational material. Second, pairs meet every few days to go over the material and solidify what was learned. Finally, the full group of four could get together to review and practice at retrieval once per week and just before the exam. Actual timing might vary based on the difficulty level of the material and the overall difficulty of the course. I have worked with many students over many years, and the following are a few strategies that have proved most helpful when forming study groups:

- Identify group members based on what needs to be accomplished, not because you like them or are friends. This is a work group, not a social group.
- Make sure everyone in the group knows the goal of the group session. Identify the content and process for each meeting.
- Prepare ahead of time. Typically, group time is not for learning foundational material. It is for reviewing, figuring out challenging material, and expanding knowledge.
- Break up the material and take turns teaching in each group session. Teaching is the best way to learn.
- Find a comfortable, public space in which the group can meet, such as a study room at the library. Private spaces like apartments can be uncomfortable for some individuals.

As with every time you study, studying in a group is a perfect time to try out your metacognitive strategies to monitor learning. Finally, be proactive. Don't wait for the professor to assign study groups. Also, don't wait to be invited. Talk to classmates, find individuals who are serious about learning, and then develop an effective strategy.

An Estimate of How Much Time to Spend Studying

The college credit hour was established a long time ago (Shedd, 2003). Here's a bit of detail that won't appear in most course catalogs: Credit hours in a course are assigned based on both the time you spend in class (an hour on the clock, minus 10 minutes for a break) *and* how much you are expected to work outside of class on average across the semester (standard of 2 hours out-of-class work for every hour spent in class). In other words, each "credit hour" is 3 hours of your week. A 3-credit hour course is designed to take 9 hours of time per week. For example:

PSYCH 101, SECTION A (3.0 credit hours): MWF, 9:00 a.m.– 9:50 a.m.

You will spend 3 hours in the classroom (there is an understood 10-minute break per hour; so, 50 minutes, three times a week or two times per week at 75 minutes per class). You'll spend 6 hours (2 hours outside work per 1 hour of in-class time) working outside of class. That's a total of 9 hours out of your week.

SPORT 101 (1.0 credit hours), MWF, 10:00 a.m.–10:50 a.m.

In this course, you spend 3 hours in class a week, but no outside work is expected. As a result, the 1 credit hour of time is all in class, which means 3 hours out of your week.

This is why 12 credit hours is considered a full-time load. That's 36 hours of work, in a country where the standard work week is 40 hours.

I explain this to show you that college classes assume a significant amount of work outside of the class period and to show why professors assign the amount of work that they do. If you really want to ace your college experience and do well on exams, papers, and other assignments, plan your week out so that you study every day for every class. Many students do not study this much. That is their choice. I suggest you make a schedule and try this out. You will be amazed at how much you can learn from each course, how well you will do on exams, and how much less stressful the course will be.

Memorize Bloom's Taxonomy

Bloom's cognitive taxonomy was devised as a way to think about how deeply something is thought about and used (Anderson & Krathwohl, 2000; Armstrong, 2010; Figure 8.1).

College faculty frequently use this taxonomy when setting class outcomes and objectives, but it can also be a helpful learning tool. Take a few minutes to study this taxonomy, and then review it once per day until the main headings become automatic: remember, understand, apply, analyze, evaluate, and create.

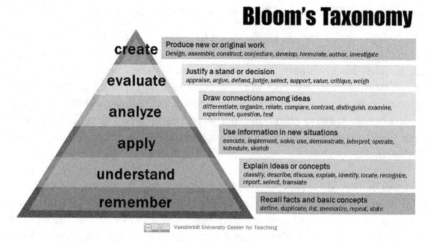

FIGURE 8.1   Bloom's Taxonomy.

Source: Armstrong (2010).

The definitions of each level are also listed, but memorize just the names of each level. I suspect that you will have this memorized within a day or two. Then review it once per week (spaced practice) until you know it well.

Study Tip 8.2: Seriously, memorize the six levels of Bloom's taxonomy.

Remember means you can call something to mind. That's it. Suppose you are asked to remember the word "chiliad" for a quiz. The next day, you write it down for the quiz. At this point, you likely don't know what it means or how it might be used in a sentence. You just remembered the word. Say you look up the word "chiliad" and find out it means "a thousand of something." Being able to explain something means you are at the *understand* level. If someone asks you how to use the word, they are asking you to *apply* it. If you research the word's origin, you have moved to the *analyze* level because you can break the word down and know what the root of the word means. If you decide that "Chiliad is an interesting word and can refer to time, but I prefer 'millennium,'" congratulations, you have hit the *evaluate* level. The final level would be *create*, where you could identify a new way to use the word or an adaptation that would add meaning to the word. You could decide to use chiliad to mean, "What you just said is 1,000 times better than anything else." With your newly created usage for the word, you might say, "Let's go hang at the park. It's chiliad this time of day."

Bloom's taxonomy will help you with learning. As you study, push concepts up the taxonomy. Imagine that "audience analysis" is introduced in Speech Communication. First learn the definition of *audience analysis* (*remember*), find out what the concept means (*understand*), and then use it in a sentence or think about how it fits into an existing schema you have (*application*).

You don't need to go to the top of the taxonomy for everything but do reach *apply* as often as you can. When you take exams, watch what kinds of questions your professor likes to ask and see if there is a pattern to the types you are getting wrong. For example, you might notice that you are getting all the *remember*- and *understand*-level questions correct. However, you may also realize that your answers to *application* and *analysis* questions are often wrong. By knowing Bloom's taxonomy, you now understand how to study for the next test. Without the taxonomy, if you get a D+ on a test, you might simply decide to "study harder." The problem with a general concept of studying harder is that there is no way to know where you should focus, and, as a result, you will likely end up wasting energy. If there is one thing I have always emphasized with my students, it is to study smarter, not harder.

Learn Every Day and Avoid Procrastination

Studying (or working on a paper, writing a lab report, reading, practicing the French horn, etc.) a small amount every day is a powerful learning strategy. As has been noted multiple times in this book, spacing study time out is very helpful in learning material that stays in long-term memory. As a powerful addition to spaced practice, teaching others has been shown time and again to be very effective (e.g., Koh et al., 2018). At the end of every learning session, explain the main findings to a roommate, friend, parent, or someone on the subway. If no humans are available, teach a cat, dog, or fish. If no pets are available, teach the major concepts to a chair or sofa. You can teach generative artificial intelligence (GenAI) the concept and request that it ask you follow-up questions that you must also explain. Then ask GenAI if you taught the topic well. The point is to teach the newly learned material as soon as possible.

Study Tip 8.3: The best way to learn anything is to teach it.

You may fall behind in studying due to procrastination, even though you know it is better not to delay the work. Research has found that up to 90% of college students procrastinate, and 50% indicate that procrastination is a problem (Steel, 2007). Avoiding procrastination is extremely important. Researchers from Griffith University have had success with low-intensity, high-frequency interventions in first-year college students (Wessel et al., 2020). They found that it was valuable for students to set small, frequent, low-stakes goals and do their best to meet them. I have seen this supported in the behavior modification courses I teach. Most individuals find it helpful to have a small, initial goal with add-on goals. For example, if you would like to read eight pages, but find that challenging, set an initial goal to read three pages. If that goes well, read an additional five pages. If you can avoid procrastination, your academic life will be much easier. Oh, and I can tell you from my students' and my own experiences that if you think you do your best work at the last minute under pressure, you are wrong. If you are good under pressure, you will be phenomenal given more time. Professionals often create something and then set it aside for a day or two and come back to it after having a bit of time to give it a fresh look.

Solicit and Incorporate Feedback

Maintaining a growth mindset is an integral part of becoming a stronger student and setting up good habits that will assist you throughout college and your entire work career. For a growth-minded person, feedback is like a road map for improving. Look for feedback anywhere you can get it. The primary source will be your professor. If you have an opportunity to look over your exams, see what kinds of multiple-choice questions (Bloom's taxonomy) you answered incorrectly and review any comments on short-answer and essay questions. The grade you receive on a test is helpful to see how you did overall, but it offers little guidance as to what specifically to change for the next test. Over the years, many of my students have looked at their overall test grades on their tests and never looked at what they missed or why. Amazingly, some of those students achieved nearly identical scores across all five exams across the entire semester. However, the students who studied their exams and found patterns in what they missed (mostly analysis questions, or mostly creation questions, or mostly multiple-choice questions) and sought feedback on how to make adjustments often got higher scores on each subsequent exam. The same can be said about term papers. Without looking carefully at your professor's feedback, you won't become a better writer.

The writing center will also typically read papers and give you feedback. Many students use the services provided in campus writing centers, so it's rare to get immediate feedback on your work. Be sure to plan for this in advance. If you are not procrastinating, you should be able to give them the first draft several weeks before the paper is due. If you can go through two or three drafts, your papers will be much better. If you have a roommate, friend, or parent who is good at writing, they are another excellent source of feedback.

GenAI and Chatbots

It is going to be a challenge to keep up with GenAI and how it can be used in educational settings (e.g., Karan & Angadi, 2023). For an idea as to how fast this area is moving, check out the website "There Is an AI for That" (https:// theresanaiforthat.com). I strongly suggest that you stay knowledgeable about what GenAI and chatbots can do but also keep in mind that this technology is a tool and should not be used to think for you. If you do not learn foundational material and learn how to think critically and creatively, you will never develop the ability to think on your own later. Consider individuals who live completely sedentary lives and never exercise. If they find themselves in a physically demanding situation, they are in trouble. You can't use a part of the human system that has not been developed. Don't let AI think for you, or you will not be able to think when you need it.

A few general considerations to keep in mind (OpenAI, 2024):

- AI should be used to help you to learn, but you yourself must have a solid understanding of the course material in the area you are studying to successfully progress to higher levels of courses and understanding.
- Understand that AI generates information from the web. It will replicate biases, prejudices, and false information that exists in the information available through an internet search.

  - Corollary: You are responsible for any final product you turn in. Check the work generated by AI.

- Be certain you understand the ethical implications of what you are using AI to do. When in doubt, ask your professor.
- Cite your source when you use AI (as I did for this section).
- Typically, whatever information you put into an AI system becomes part of the system, and the internet writes in ink. Be sure you have the right to input the information.
- Information and images may be "scraped" from sources that have not given permission to be used. Even what appears to be "original" work from AI may be plagiarized.
- It will become increasingly easy for individuals to create manufactured information. This means knowing what is real is going to require a strong critical thinking skillset very soon.

Overall, AI is going to provide extensive opportunities to help you to learn. Just be sure you are using the systems to learn and not letting the systems do the work for you.

———————•◄—————

Study Tip 8.4: Use GenAI to test and strengthen your knowledge, not to skip over foundational work. Without a strong foundation, coursework in higher-level classes will become increasingly difficult.

———————•◄—————

Office of Student Success/Student Disability Services

Just over 9% (about 1 million) of students at 4-year institutions report having at least one disability. About 12% (about 700,000) of students at 2-year institutions report having disabilities (NCES, 2017). Although these numbers are high, keep in mind there are many additional individuals who either don't report their disability or don't know they have one. Every institution in higher education has an office to assist students with disabilities, whether online or on-site, 2-year or 4-year, public or private, at no charge to their students. These offices may be called Disability Resources, Accessibility Resources, Student Accessibility Services, or another name. A quick search on your campus website should bring up the center. Faculty attitudes regarding accommodations for both physical and mental disabilities tend to be favorable to neutral (Banks, 2019), meaning that faculty are not rarely frustrated or angry when providing accommodations.

Unfortunately, we have an educational system that was founded on equality, where everyone is treated the same, rather than equity, where everyone is given what they need (note: not necessarily what they *want*) to move forward. Treating everyone the same (i.e., equality) works when everyone arrives with the same resources. Unfortunately, not everyone arrives at the same level, and in many cases, it is totally outside the person's control. One example of equity is a person with clinical depression who may be allowed more excused absences, because there will be times when they will not be physically able to get to campus. Everyone getting the same number of excused days is equal, but not equitable, because some people need more, through no fault of their own.

Higher education is built for healthy, risk-taking, fast-talking extroverts. Those individuals have a considerable advantage. Students who do not fit that description, such as those who are deaf, on the autism spectrum, have a brain injury, psychiatric disorder, learning disability, chronic health issue(s), or attention deficit disorder may find it nearly impossible to get a degree without accommodations. The general rules of the educational game are stacked against them. If you had accommodations in high school, if you think you might have a disability, or if you study very hard and still can't seem to "get" the material, visit your campus's disability student services. Allow plenty of time, because accommodations cannot be granted on the day they are requested. There is a process to ensure you get the accommodations you *need*, although you may not get all that you *want*. The reason for accommodations is to provide individuals with an opportunity to earn a degree. Nothing is being "given" to them. Be mindful that all accommodations must come from the office of disability student services. Faculty members are not allowed to give accommodations without the proper documentation.

Chapter Summary

Many aspects of being a successful student are "hidden" components, known to those who have learned from someone who attended college. Those who are not told, for whatever reason, are at a disadvantage when it comes to being a successful student. Deciding when to study alone (in a pair or in a group) is valuable, particularly when done with growth-mindedness and metacognitive skills. Courses are built with the expectation that you will study for 2 hours outside of class for each hour in class, providing ample time to learn the material and be prepared for class. As you study, keep Bloom's taxonomy in mind to determine how deeply you are learning inside and outside the classroom. Part of keeping up with coursework and finishing papers on time is to keep doing some work every day. However, procrastination impacts learning for many students, and if you tend to procrastinate, it will be essential to identify strategies to keep procrastination to a minimum. Another aspect of college life that is rarely discussed is making good use of feedback. Feedback can be a road map to doing better in the future. Being a strong student will also help keep you out of a situation where you might feel the need to cheat or plagiarize. It is critical to differentiate when GenAI is helpful from when it is unhelpful and potentially academically dangerous to use. If you qualify for accommodations, be sure to use them as they are there to help level the playing field and give you a legitimate opportunity to graduate with a college degree.

Discussion Questions

1   Do you tend to prefer to study alone or in groups? Based on how you study, what would be a good way for you to balance individual and group studying?
2   Identify something you have recently learned that you can explain at each level of Bloom's taxonomy. Explain it as though you were teaching someone to use the pyramid of cognitive levels.
3   Do you tend to procrastinate? Select either 3a or 3b, based on your situation.

    3a   If so, explain why you think you typically procrastinate. What are some strategies you might try to reduce the amount of time you procrastinate?
    3b   If you don't procrastinate, what are strategies you use to keep from procrastinating? Do you schedule time, turn your phone off, and so on? Explain as though you are helping a procrastinator get started.

4   In what ways have you found GenAI to be helpful to you in your academic learning? What concerns do you have with respect to GenAI in both college and society at large?

References

Anderson, L. W., & Krathwohl, D. R. (2000). *A taxonomy for learning, teaching, and assessing—A revision of Bloom's taxonomy of educational objectives*. Allyn & Bacon.

Armstrong, P. (2010). *Bloom's taxonomy*. Vanderbilt University Center for Teaching. https://cft.vanderbilt.edu/guides-sub-pages/blooms-taxonomy/

Banks, J. (2019). Are we ready: Faculty perceptions of postsecondary students with learning disabilities at a historically Black University. *Journal of Diversity in Higher Education, 12*(4), 297–306. https://doi.org/10.1037/dhe0000100

Jackson, P. W. (1990). *Life in classrooms*. Holt, Rinehart, and Winston.

Karan, B., & Angadi, G. R. (2023). Potential risks of artificial intelligence integration into school education: A systematic review. *Bulletin of Science, Technology, & Society, 43*(3–4), 67–85. https://doi.org/10.1177/02704676231224705

Kelly, A. V. (2009). *The curriculum: Theory and practice* (6th ed.). SAGE.

Kim, N. J., Belland, B. R., Mason, L., Lindi, A., Walker, A., & Axelrod, D. (2020). Computer-based scaffolding targeting individual versus groups in problem-centered instruction for STEM education: Meta-analysis. *Educational Psychology Review, 32*(2), 415–461. http://dx.doi.org/10.1007/s10648-019-09502-3

Koh, A. W. L., Lee, S. C., & Lim, S. W. H. (2018). The learning benefits of teaching: A retrieval practice hypothesis. *Applied Cognitive Psychology, 32*(3), 401–410. https://doi.org/10.1002/acp.3410

National Center for Education Statistics. (2017). *Characteristics and outcomes of undergraduates with disabilities*. U.S. Department of Education. https://nces.ed.gov/pubs2018/2018432.pdf

OpenAI (2024, February 17). *Guidelines for college students using generative AI for coursework*. ChatGPT 3.5. OpenAI. https://chat.openai.com/c/a19b983b-266b-4d44-b8d3-9e55bb7ac1e7

Shedd, J. M. (2003). The history of the student credit hour. In J. V. Wellman & T. Erlich (Eds.), *How the student credit hour shapes higher education: The tie that binds* (*New directions for higher education*, no. 122, pp. 5–12). Jossey-Bass. http://dx.doi.org/10.1002/he.106

Steel, P. (2007). The nature of procrastination: A meta-analytic and theoretical review of quintessential self-regulatory failure. *Psychological Bulletin, 133*(1), 65–94. https://doi.org/10.1037/0033-2909.133.1.65

Wessel, J., Bradley, G. L., & Hood, M. (2020). A low-intensity, high-frequency intervention to reduce procrastination. *Applied Psychology, 70*(4), 1669–1690. https://doi.org/10.1111/apps.12293

9
AVOIDING LEARNING PITFALLS

College is a place to try new things and, at times, make mistakes you will learn from. If you never make mistakes, then you are likely not trying new things that push you to new levels. The challenge is to avoid *pitfalls*, "a hidden or not easily recognized danger or difficulty" (Merriam-Webster, n.d.). When the danger, difficulty, or mistake has the potential to seriously impact educational progress, I call those *learning pitfalls*. This chapter covers six common learning pitfalls and ways to circumvent them. I have seen students seriously impacted by each of the following, and unfortunately, experienced enough of these that I needed an extra year to complete my undergraduate degree in psychology.

Learning Pitfall #1: Ineffective Study Strategies

Highlighting and rereading without a specific purpose are common "study" strategies that don't work (Dunlosky et al., 2013). I think students run into this pitfall because of tradition and a false sense of how people learn. Tradition is apparent in used textbooks with bands of fluorescent colors (Blasiman et al., 2016). Highlighting while reading a dense chapter makes many students feel like they are learning. Unfortunately, that isn't how learning works. Highlighting is like walking through a museum and glancing at the art. In a matter of seconds, while in a room full of items an interesting piece is noted, and then it is on to the next interesting piece. It feels like you have seen the collection, but later it's challenging to recall many, if any, specifics about the collection as a whole. That is how highlighting in textbooks typically works. Reading along, selecting something that catches one's attention, and then moving on to the next bit of material.

DOI: 10.4324/9781003499176-12

Rereading is also a commonly used study strategy in college (Morehead et al., 2015), and much like highlighting, it also brings about a false sense of learning (Weinstein et al., 2010). Seeing something multiple times *can* lead to learning, but only if you process the information. For example, you've likely handled a lot of U.S. coins over the past 10 or 15 years. Take a moment, draw a circle, and then sketch what is on the front of a quarter, including any words. If you are studying with friends, you can make a competition of it. Compare your drawing to an actual quarter. How close were you? Seeing something, even hundreds of times, without processing the information is not enough to get it into your memory.

Study Tip 9.1: Always read with a purpose and check for focus as you read. If you are rereading material, this is even more important.

With a bit of modification, though, highlighting and rereading *can* "work." Dunlosky and colleagues at Kent State University—the team who noted that highlighting and rereading are often not effective—also observed that strategies that involve encoding and elaboration (see Chapter 4) *are* effective (Dunlosky et al., 2013). So, make sure you are encoding and elaborating the information when you use any study strategy. The essential step is to mentally process the information in some way. Write a note about why it's important, turn the highlighted text into a short question, or reread for a specific purpose.

Avoiding Pitfall #1: If you are going to reread and highlight, be sure to build in cognitively engaging strategies. For example, because remembering is not enough to cognitively engage with the material, create your own questions based on the highlighted material that are at Bloom's taxonomy level of understanding or above.

Learning Pitfall #2: Cheating and Plagiarism

You know what kind of person you are, so this section is not a lecture on the importance of integrity. What I can do here is help you avoid situations that can lead to the desperation that often results in cheating and also help keep you from unknowingly cheating.

Cheating

There are many ways to get yourself into a jam where you might be more likely to consider cheating on an exam, homework, or assignment. The following are frequent causes of student cheating (Eberly Center, n.d.):

- Being unprepared
- Fearing failure
- Poor study skills
- Fierce competition to earn and maintain a high GPA
- Feeling that the professor is unfair or the assignment is unreasonable
- A social obligation to help others to cheat
- A perceived lack of consequences for cheating
- A feeling of anonymity in class

Note that these are reported causes, *not* acceptable justifications for cheating on an assignment, quiz, or exam. In my experience, being unprepared, whether because students simply didn't study or they didn't know how to study effectively, is the biggest cause of cheating. Use the strategies in this book and in this chapter to avoid being unprepared. Even if it happens that you don't prepare as well as you could have, it's better to figure out how to recover from a bad grade than to be caught cheating and risk being kicked out of school, flunking a course, and tanking your reputation. Even if the cheating happens before the class's drop period, you likely won't be able to just drop the class and move on. Colleges typically have provisions to ensure that students still receive an F as punishment for cheating.

Plagiarism

Faculty have different definitions of *plagiarism*, particularly concerning paraphrasing (Blum, 2009; Lang, 2015). The most common definition boils down to using anyone's work without giving them proper credit. This includes using content created by AI. It is a best practice to give credit to *any* work you use and cite the work in the style being used in your class: Chicago, MLA, APA, or AMA.

One writing strategy that I always give students to help them avoid even accidental plagiarism (yes, accidental plagiarism can happen, and, yes, you will be punished even if you didn't mean to plagiarize): Jot down the gist of the information you want to use *and* the citation from where it came. Then, when you write your paper, expand on what you already put down in your words and be sure to include the citation immediately. This will make sure it is in your words and you have given credit to the person writing the original material from where you drew your ideas. Most professionals agree that it is a *terrible* idea to be looking at the actual source while writing or to cut and paste the part you intend to use into your paper with the idea of putting it into your own words later.

Academic misconduct is a very serious and very complex concept. If you have any uncertainty about what is okay and what is not, go to the academic success or writing center or ask your professor.

Avoiding Pitfall #2: Don't put yourself in a situation that increases the likeli-hood of feeling you must cheat. Cite any work by others, and if you have any uncertainty, ask how and when you should cite work.

Learning Pitfall #3: Following Your Learning Style

Two researchers from a medical school in the United Kingdom reviewed 37 studies involving more than 15,000 teachers from 18 countries and found that nearly 90% of teachers believe in matching instruction to learning styles (Newton & Salvi, 2020). Unfortunately, this is a huge learning pitfall. People love the idea of discovering something new about themselves that can be used for good. Teachers like the idea of teaching the best way possible to meet the needs of each individual student. Who wouldn't want that? It turns out that *no* data show that teaching in a way that matches a learning style results in better learning (Dekker et al., 2020; Pashler et al., 2008).

This pitfall is based on a misunderstanding that most people miss, even though it is right out in the open. Parents, teachers, and students mistakenly hear that they can find out *how* they learn, even though most learning style promoters are careful to say that they'll reveal how you *prefer* to learn. There is a significant difference between these, particularly if you mistakenly believe that "how you *prefer* to learn" means it is difficult to learn any other way. An added problem is that learning style advocates love boxing you into being a visual learner, an auditory learner, or a kinesthetic learner. When someone takes a learning styles inventory, it is very rare to be 100% in any one area. You may be 45% visual, 30% auditory, and 25% kinesthetic, in which case you would be labeled a visual learner, because that's your largest percentage. It would be like eating 55% sal-ads and 45% meats and being told you are a vegetarian.

Study Tip 9.2: Don't always learn the way that you think you prefer. Experiment with other ways to see what else works well for you in differ-ent situations.

The best way to learn is to match how you will retrieve information with how you should encode it. If you are going to identify paintings, it is best to look at paintings. If you are learning to write short stories, it is best to read and write short stories. That is how learning really works. Want to confirm this? Search "learning style myth" in your favorite search engine.

Avoiding Pitfall #3: Don't let pseudoscience lead you away from strategies to improve your learning. If your professor does not teach in a way you *prefer* to learn (note: *prefer*, not *can* learn), you can build the skills you need to process what is given and search out resources that will help you succeed.

Learning Pitfall #4: Task Shifting

Task shifting is when we direct our attention away from one task and shift to another. The problem is that every time you shift, you lose information, because it takes your brain a bit of time to reorient itself. Glancing at your phone while reading does not just cost you the time of looking at your phone; it also costs you the time it takes for your brain to get back into what you were reading. Even worse, until you solidify information, the memory trace is very susceptible to interference (Chapter 5). When you text someone while reading, you weaken the memory of the information you just read.

Task shifting is not multitasking; everyone can multitask. It would be absolutely awful if we could not multitask. We can walk and carry on a conversation, drive while listening to music, and eat while reading the latest news on our phones. That said, we can't multitask everything. Things like texting (or shopping on laptops) and listening to a lecture at the same time are nearly impossible. In such situations, we are really task shifting, which means we text a little (while not listening to the lecture) then shift to listening to the lecture (while not texting) and then back again. The pitfall is that your brain gets just enough information to trick you into thinking that you are "getting" what is being discussed in class, but it comes with two dangers. The first is cognitive cost. The process of shifting takes a bit of energy every time you shift, because you must figure out quickly what was missed (Strayer et al., 2022). The second is what you miss without realizing. If you are fast, you may be able to send a text in about 5 seconds. It takes about 3–5 seconds to read a text. Five seconds might not seem long, but imagine 10 seconds of not paying attention while you are driving. Time for an experiment. Set your phone timer for 10 seconds and pretend you are driving. Close your eyes as you hit "Start" on your timer and wait until you hear the tone indicating the 10 seconds are over. Driving while texting is the same as having your eyes closed. If you were in a vehicle going 60 miles per hour, in 10 seconds you would have just driven the distance of two football fields, with your eyes closed.

This danger is the same on the lecture side of task shifting. If you are texting someone during lecture, you might stop paying attention for perhaps 15 seconds (although it is likely longer). What if your professor said, "Here are three things you should never do when setting up an experiment, and 5 seconds later you finish your text and look up? Your brain missed that warning of what *not* to do. All you hear and interpret is three things about running an experiment. In a case such as this, a pitfall can happen in the few seconds you are focused elsewhere and miss that these are "don't do" rather than "do"! I have watched students get so engrossed in texting that they missed nearly everything in a class period.

Task shifting when studying is also a pitfall. A text conversation might cost you only 5 minutes, but 5 minutes here and there add up, and hours are lost. If you text periodically while studying or reading, it disrupts your flow and greatly decreases your learning. When studying, block off time—say 30 minutes—set a timer on your phone and then place the phone on airplane mode or mute, and study with focus until the timer rings. Because you have a timer set, you don't need to check the clock to see if 30 minutes is up. If you are on your laptop and getting distracted, turn the Wi-Fi off. During a timed, planned study break, check your phone or your email, and then get back to studying.

It is also important to note that smartphone addiction is increasingly becoming a global concern. Overuse of smartphones is linked to worse physical health, sleep disorders, and psychological challenges such as anxiety, depression, loneliness, and impaired concentration. All of these things impact learning in a negative way. A study in China noted cell phone addiction in nearly 40% of college students. The good news is that reducing cell phone use reduces the negative side effects of excessive cell phone use (Mei et al., 2023).

Smartphones have been popular for only about 10 years. Before smartphones and cell towers were abundant, people lived their lives without having connections to their friends, family, and the world of TikTok in the palm of their hand, and now I catch myself carrying my phone from room to room when I move about my house. Recently I have been taking walks without my phone, and I admit that at first it made me nervous. Then I realized that if I can't be without something for 20–30 minutes without feeling nervous, that's basically the definition of dependency and addiction.

> **Avoiding Pitfall #4:** In class and while studying, put your phone away and mute social notifications. Researchers at Michigan State University found that task shifting is highly dependent on habits, so create good habits (Kononova & Yuan, 2017). *Subpitfall*: Take breaks from your smartphone for the health of it.

Learning Pitfall #5: Hanging in There Too Long

This pitfall pertains to trying save a course that can't be saved. There are times when things just won't go in your favor, and, whatever the cause, a class is simply not going to end well. Despite this, some students grimly hang on and finish out a course with a grade that tanks their GPA because they put time into studying for the course that couldn't be saved instead of shifting focus to the courses still in play. One reason students fall into this pitfall is because of *sunk cost*, a term often used in psychology and economics. Once you have committed resources (sunk cost), decisions after that point should generally be based on the upcoming circumstances, not what you've already put in. You're not going to get those resources (time, money, sleep) back, whatever you do. However, humans don't tend to do that well, resulting in the *sunk cost fallacy* (or *sunk cost effect*), which happens when sunk cost expenses drive future actions.

Here is an example in my life where I used this information to avoid a sunk cost fallacy. My wife, daughter, and I went to a symphony concert. We paid $50 each for the three tickets. We were caught in a sudden downpour walking from the parking garage across the street into the music hall, and the three of arrived at the building absolutely soaked, dripping puddles, and freezing in the air-conditioned hall. We could have said, "I spent $150 for these tickets, so we are staying." However, we understood the concept of sunk cost. The $150 was gone (sunk cost), so the question was really: If the tickets had been free, would we have sat in drenched clothes, freezing? We chatted quickly, unanimously said no, and quietly got up and left.

That's not to say you shouldn't consider cost at all. If you have completed 3 years of college and find yourself frustrated and tired of school in the fourth year, you might think about quitting. But the amount of work and money invested (sunk cost) encourages you to finish, to find motivation to do the work. That is when sunk cost is helpful.

The pitfall comes from not realizing when or if the consequences of continuing outweigh the cost invested. I have worked with students in my classes who needed to drop the course but would not do so. They often said that they had so much energy invested in the course that they just wanted to make it to the end. Even after I explained to them that there was no way that they could pass, sometimes they would say they just wanted to finish. As a result, they spent time studying for a class they couldn't pass instead of reallocating that valuable time for other courses. Unfortunately, they got caught by the "hanging in there too long" pitfall.

Avoiding Pitfall #5: I am hopeful everything goes great for every class you have, but if it doesn't, don't give up just because a course is challenging. If you can succeed, put in the energy and stick with it even though it is unpleasant. However, if it is mathematically (or physically, emotionally, logistically, etc.) impossible to succeed, then talk to an advisor or your faculty about dropping the course. Do watch for other costs, particularly if dropping a course puts you at less than full-time, in which case you could lose scholarships or even your status as a full-time student.

Learning Pitfall #6: Not Using Campus Resources

It may not feel like it all the time, but once you are enrolled, colleges are set up to do everything they can to help you be successful. They do care about you, and they also keep statistics on graduations in which it is important they show student success. So, in addition to caring about you as a person, they care about you graduating, which is good for everyone. As a result, there are many resources on college campuses available to you, and they are typically already paid for by your tuition.

How can you find out what's available? There are college student orientation sessions, web resources, faculty advisors, dorm advisors, peer networks in living/learning communities (LCs), and much more (Grim et al., 2021). Grim and colleagues at the University of Michigan found that peers, LCs, and faculty advisors were particularly good sources of information. There may even be a group chat or GroupMe you can join.

Study Tip 9.4: It doesn't matter how well you are doing, find resources to make your learning even better.

Three points are critically important when it comes to campus resources. First, almost all resources are included with your tuition, so you have already paid for them and there is usually no additional charge for using campus resources. Second, these resources are there to help you. Never worry about "bothering" anyone by availing yourself of those resources or asking multiple people to find the answer you need. Third, there are likely many more resources on campus than you realize and at times more than professors realize. Most students need assistance at some point, and it is a safe assumption that if you need assistance with something, others do too, and an office on campus offers it. If you feel unwell, there is a health center or counseling center; if you are struggling academically, there are writing centers and tutor centers (tutors in nearly every discipline). Some campuses even have programs designed specifically for students on academic probation. See Table 9.1 for the names of resource centers and offices that are found on college campuses. Not every campus will have all the centers and offices on this list, and the names of the centers may be different. Explore your institution's website or ask your instructor to see what's there. I offer this list only to get you thinking about possibilities.

Also note that many of these services are helpful for individuals who are not having academic difficulty. The writing center is a great resource for students who are getting high grades. As a faculty member, I have visited writing centers to ask about an aspect of my writing.

Avoiding Pitfall #6: There are great campus resources available for everyone taking courses at the college. Use them.

TABLE 9.1 Examples of resource centers and offices

Advising	Bookstore	Career Center
Childcare Center	Computer Lab	Counseling Center
Crisis Centers	Cultural Studies	Disability Student Services
Diversity and Intercultural Life	Financial Aid/Short-Term Loan	Fitness/Athletic Center
Food Bank/Pantry	Health Services	Information Technology
International Students	Internships	Legal Services
LGBTQIA+ Office	Library	Math Help Center
Multicultural Center	Pre-Graduate School Advising	Printing Centers
Public Safety	Road to Resilience	Safe Space
Spiritual Life Office	Student Services	Transfer Center
Tutoring	Undergraduate Research	Veteran's Resources
Writing Center		

Chapter Summary

In this chapter, I presented six learning pitfalls that can negatively impact student success, along with suggestions for dealing with them. I have seen students get into trouble with every one of these pitfalls, every semester. These dangers are not always easily recognized. Students have been reading and highlighting for a very long time, often with an elevated false sense of learning. It crushes me when students find themselves in a situation where they feel the need to cheat on a test, buy a paper, have a GenAI program write a paper, or plagiarize the work of others. Cheating has huge consequences, including losing scholarships and even being kicked out of college.

Learning style is a myth that continues to be perpetuated. We do have learning preferences, but we don't require a specific way to learn. Task shifting has a large impact on learning. Limiting loss of information by staying focused can keep you on more solid ground. Another topic not discussed enough is centered around knowing when to hold and knowing when to fold. Unfortunately, some situations are just not going to work out. Sometimes, the best way to handle something is to walk away and avoid the sunk cost fallacy. Finally, there are so many campus resources available to all students. Find what is possible and make good use of them.

Discussion Questions

1 Explain how bringing elaboration into the highlighting process would increase the effectiveness of this strategy. Describe a way (other than the example used in this chapter) that highlighting or rereading could be made more effective.
2 Do you ever tuck your phone away to study? If so, explain the process to keep yourself from checking your phone frequently. If you don't put your phone away when you study, what could you do to ignore your device long enough to study for 1 hour?
3 Go online and identify five resources that you feel would be helpful to you as a college student. Under what circumstances might you use those resources and what outcomes would you expect from them?

References

Blasiman, R. N., Dunlosky, J., & Rawson, K. A. (2016). The what, how much, and when of study strategies: Comparing intended versus actual study behaviour. *Memory*, *25*(6), 784–792. https://doi.org/10.1080/09658211.2016.1221974

Blum, S. D. (2009, February 2020). Academic integrity and student plagiarism: A question of education, not ethics. *The Chronicle of Higher Education*: *Commentary*. http://www.chronicle.com/article/academic-integritystudent/32323

Dekker, S., Lee, N. C., Howard-Jones, P., & Jolles, J. (2020). Neuromyths in education: Prevalence and predictors of misconceptions among teachers. *Frontiers in Psychology*, *3*, 429. https://doi.org/10.3389/fpsyg.2012.00429

Dunlosky, J., Rawson, K. A., Marsh, E. J., Nathan, M. J., & Willingham, D. T. (2013). Improving students' learning with effective learning techniques: Promising directions from cognitive and educational psychology. *Psychological Science in the Public Interest*, *14*(1), 4–58. https://doi.org/10.1177/1529100612453266

Eberly Center. (n.d.). *Students cheat on assignments and exams*. Carnegie Mellon University. http://www.cmu.edu/teaching/solveproblem/strat-cheating/index.html

Grim, J. K., Bausch, E., Hussain, A., & Lonn, S. (2021). Is it what you know or who you know? An information typology of how first-generation college students access campus resources. *Journal of College Student Retention: Research, Theory, & Practice*. https://doi.org/10.1177/15210251211068115

Kononova, A. G., & Yuan, S. (2017). Take a break: Examining college students' media multitasking activities and motivations during study- or work-related tasks. *Journalism & Mass Communication Educator*, *72*(2), 183–197. https://doi.org/10.1177/1077695816649474

Lang, J. M. (2015, May 4). Cheating inadvertently. *The Chronicle of Higher Education: Advice*. http://www.chronicle.com/article/Cheating-Inadvertently/229883/

Mei, S., Hu, Y., Wu, X., Cao, R., Kong, Y., Zhang, L., Lin, X., Liu, Q., Hu, Y., & Li, L. (2023). Health risks of mobile phone addiction among college students in China. *International Journal of Mental Health and Addiction*, *21*, 2650–2665. https://doi.org/10.1007/s11469-021-00744-3

Merriam-Webster. (n.d.). *Pitfall*. In Merriam-Webster.com Dictionary. https://www.merriam-webster.com/dictionary/pitfall

Morehead, K., Rhodes, M. G., & DeLozier, S. (2015). Instructor and student knowledge of study strategies. *Memory, 24*(2), 257–271. https://doi.org/10.1080/09658211.2014.1001992

Newton, P. M., & Salvi, A. (2020). How common is belief in the learning styles neuromyth, and does it matter? A pragmatic systematic review. *Frontiers in Education, 5*, 602451. https://doi.org/10.3389/feduc.2020.602451

Pashler, H., McDaniel, M., Rohrer, D., & Bjork, R. (2008). Learning styles: Concepts and evidence. *Psychological Science in the Public Interest, 9*(3), 105–119. https://doi.org/10.1111/j.1539-6053.2009.01038.x

Strayer, D. L., Castro, S. C., Turrill, J., & Cooper, J. M. (2022). The persistence of distraction: The hidden costs of intermittent multitasking. *Journal of Experimental Psychology: Applied*. Advance online publication. https://doi.org/10.1037/xap0000388

Weinstein, Y., McDermott, K. B., & Roediger, H. L. (2010). A comparison of study strategies for passages: Rereading, answering questions, and generating questions. *Journal of Experimental Psychology: Applied, 16*(3), 308–316. https://doi.org/10.1037/a0020992

PART 4

Keep It Going

10

SLEEPING TO ENHANCE LEARNING

You know how great a good night of sleep can be, and you know that very few people look in the mirror after a terrible night of sleep and say, "Wow, I look fantastic and it's going to be a great day." What you may not realize is the extent to which sleep deprivation impacts mood, relationships, academic performance, and many aspects of health. The Centers for Disease Control and Prevention (CDC, 2016) reported that individuals getting fewer than 7 hours per night over an extended period are at higher risk for developing health challenges such as "obesity, diabetes, high blood pressure, heart disease, stroke, and frequent mental distress" (para. 2).

I fully understand that due to life circumstances, you may not have the opportunity to get a healthy amount of sleep. As a full-time undergraduate student, I had to work around 40 hours per week to cover the cost of tuition and living expenses, and getting a full night of sleep was very challenging. The key is to do the best you can with what you have. Maximize opportunities and make good use of your time to get as much sleep as possible.

What Researchers Say About Sleep

Researchers started studying sleep over 100 years ago, and there are still many things we don't know. We do know that many college students are sleep deprived. The University of Georgia (UGA) collects health data and found that most UGA students report getting between 6 and 6.9 hours of sleep each night (UGA, 2021). The National Center for Health Statistics (2017) noted that nearly 73% of high school students got fewer than 8 hours of sleep per night.

DOI: 10.4324/9781003499176-14

Stages of Sleep

When we sleep, nearly everyone proceeds through a predictable pattern of stages. There are two different sleep states: rapid eye movement (REM) sleep and nonrapid eye movement (NREM) sleep. REM sleep is important for memory consolidation and emotional regulation. Upon entering REM, muscles become atonic, which means you can't use your arms and legs, and your eyes begin to move back and forth, although eyes remain closed. This is when you dream the most, and one hypothesis is that suppression of muscle movement keeps humans from acting out their dreams. REM sleep is sometimes called paradoxical sleep because the brain is very active, almost the same as when awake, yet it can be challenging to wake someone in this state.

NREM state is divided into four stages.

Stage 1 is light sleep and typically lasts less than 7 minutes. It is easy to wake up while in this stage and can be difficult to tell if someone is asleep, just relaxed, or distracted.

Stage 2 lasts about 20 minutes. In this stage, the heart rates drop and brain waves begin to slow.

Stage 3 is a short stage and signals a move from light sleep to deeper sleep.

Stage 4 is the deepest NREM stage, where slow delta waves appear. This stage is often called deep sleep, and in the first sleep cycle of the night, it will last about 30 minutes. If someone wakes you up or an alarm clock goes off while in Stage 4, you will find it difficult to wake up. This is an important stage for many of sleeps' physiological benefits, including healing and strengthening the immune system. Memory consolidation happens during this phase—without deep Stage 4 sleep, it is easy to forget much of what was learned the day before.

Sleep cycles take about 90 minutes to complete. Under normal circumstances, most individuals go through five cycles, which is typically about 7.5 hours. As the night progresses, Stage 4 deep sleep gets shorter and REM gets longer (Carskadon & Dement, 2011). When a person is sleep deprived and finally get some sleep the body will prioritize the important parts of sleep. This means the person goes into deep sleep much faster and stays in that stage for long periods during the first few sleep cycles. A bit later in the night REM is extended. This is why it is very difficult to wake up after an hour or so when the person is sleep deprived.

Study Tip 10.1: A good night of sleep will make your study time much more efficient. We learn faster and store memories more efficiently when rested.

Sleep Patterns: Larks and Night Owls

Much has been written about people who tend to get up early, called *larks*, and those who like to stay up at night, called *owls*. It turns out most of us are a mix of the two (Jarrett, 2021). To figure out whether you are a lark or an owl, keep a log for a week of how you slept the previous night, then rate how effective you feel while doing various activities throughout the day (e.g., reading, listening to lectures, doing homework problems). A pattern will likely emerge that shows when you do your best thinking and how your sleep affects your day. The results might surprise you! I kept a log like this as an assignment when I was an undergraduate in a psychology class. I thought it was a waste of time because I was sure I knew my peak performing times. I was wrong. I like to stay up late, but it turns out I am cognitively sharpest early in the morning. I also found out that although I am active all day, I am not mentally alert between 2:00 p.m. and 4:00 p.m. To this day, I schedule my writing and research (cognitively demanding tasks) in the early morning and use midafternoon time for breaks and tasks that are less cognitively demanding, such as setting up my to-do list for the next day, lighter reading, and socializing.

Sleep, Learning, and Memory

Although sleep is necessary for the brain to function well, 70% of college students report that they don't get enough sleep (Okano et al., 2019). Researchers have found that poor sleep habits impact academic performance for students all over the world, from China (Wong et al., 2013), to Ethiopia (Lemma et al., 2014), and the United States (Gilbert & Weaver, 2010). Anyone who has been exhausted when taking a test knows that being tired makes remembering harder, thinking more clouded, and creative problem-solving more challenging.

As noted in Chapter 5, consolidation is important for long-term memory, and this typically happens during deep Stage 4 sleep. If you do not sleep relatively soon after learning something new, consolidation doesn't happen, and you likely won't remember what you learned, even if you catch up on sleep later. Pulling an all-nighter and then going to classes the next day hurts on both sides of the night. Information learned the day before the all-nighter is not consolidated well, so much of it is lost. Research also shows that when an exhausted brain encounters new information, it is challenging to learn, so information encountered the day after an all-nighter is more challenging to learn. Even if you feel fine after an all-nighter, research suggests your ability to learn is about 20% lower than if you were rested (Mander et al., 2011).

Because memory consolidation works best when sleep happens relatively soon after learning the new material (Gais et al., 2006), information learned closer to the time you go to bed will be consolidated better than information learned earlier in the day, provided you are not tired while studying. This is an important consideration for your study allocation. If you have 2 hours set aside to study, one from 10:00 a.m. to 11:00 a.m. and another from 9:00 p.m. to 10:00 p.m., it would be best to study the easier material in the morning and the more challenging material closer to when you intend to go to bed.

Remembering What Is Important During Sleep

You are exposed to millions of pieces of information through sights and sounds every minute, all day long. Some of the information you process is important, but other information is not needed, so it should be forgotten to free up cognitive space. There is no reason to remember the color of a car parked next to yours at the grocery store. Although researchers don't know exactly how it works, they do have evidence that much of the sorting of what to remember and what to forget happens while you sleep (Wilhelm et al., 2011).

For long-term learning, an expectation that information will be needed in the future is helpful, as the brain is less likely to discard information that will be needed later. An exam is undoubtedly one way to signal importance, but there are better ways. As you study, think about how this information might be used in other classes, at a job, or to help people. Learning to calculate the strength of different types of steel may seem unimportant as you study in the library, but it was significant for the construction of that library.

Power of Naps and Restful Breaks

Naps have been studied for decades across various circumstances, and the findings are consistent: Daytime naps, in some cases as short as 6 minutes, significantly improve learning (Farhadian et al., 2021).

Many people choose to take a nap for an hour, which does not work well with how sleep cycles flow. One hour after going to sleep, you are likely in Stage 4, which makes it hard to wake up. When you do, you are groggy and irritated. Or perhaps you didn't get up after the 1 hour and ended up sleeping much longer than you had anticipated? That is the challenge with waking up in Stage 4.

It is best to nap less than 20 minutes or around 90 minutes. A short nap will put you in Stage 2 when it is time to wake up, which is easy to do. If you have more time, it is best to nap for about 90 minutes, as that will let you sleep one complete cycle and put you back near Stage 1, making it much easier for you to wake up and feel refreshed.

Research on naps has been done all over the world. In Singapore, a group that napped after learning word pairs outperformed a group that watched a video after learning the word pairs (Ong et al., 2020). Research also shows that you don't have to take a nap to get refreshed. If you don't have time to nap, you can still take a restful break by closing your eyes and relaxing. Research shows these short breaks are helpful in keeping the new information intact. Children given a restful break recalled one-third more words on a vocabulary list than children in a control group who watched a video (Martini et al., 2019).

Cramming Versus Resting

I have asked college students all over the country if cramming is an effective study strategy. As you likely know, most say that it is not effective. Then I ask how many students cram for exams the night before the test. This response will not surprise you either: About 90% of the same students who just said it was not a good idea say they cram for exams.

Study Tip 10.2: Regularly spaced-out study sessions are much better than cramming. As a bonus, there will be less stress the night before the test and less cognitive fuzziness during the test.

The good news is that you are in a very select group of individuals who know why cramming does not work (see Chapter 5). You also know a bit of research from this chapter on naps and rests, so you know how to study smarter in harmony with your brain.

Managing Your Sleep

Because of its importance, whenever you are behind on sleep, your body will spend more time in deep, slow-wave sleep and REM than usual. The result is that you can make up *some* sleep deprivation with just a bit of extra sleep. But don't make a habit of it. Many people rack up sleep debt every week and then sleep a bit longer on the weekends in an attempt to get out of debt. Research suggests this is not a great idea. Smith and a team of colleagues from the University of Pennsylvania, Virginia Tech, and the Johnson Space Center collaborated on a study pertaining to sleep debt at the NASA Human Exploration Research Analog (HERA) in Houston, Texas (Smith et al., 2021). The researchers kept participants in a simulated spacecraft for 45 days. During this time, the participants slept in a pattern of five shorter weekday nights (accumulating debt) followed by two longer weekend nights (making up for the debt). Results showed that individuals in the experimental group who slept less during the week and slept large amounts over the weekend to catch up demonstrated significantly lower performance on cognitive tests and attention tasks.

·Factors That Disrupt Sleep

Following are some common causes of sleep disruption for college students. As always, there are variations between people, and there can even be variations within people at different times.

Alcohol Consumption

Because people get excited, yell, and are animated while drinking, many think alcohol is a stimulant. Not true. Alcohol is a central nervous system depressant and has a negative impact on several aspects of sleep, depending on age, physical shape, biological sex, and food consumption. Because alcohol disrupts sleep, it also disrupts learning the formation of new memories (Pietilä et al., 2018).

Caffeine

Caffeine is the most widely consumed psychoactive drug globally, and many people depend on it to get them going in the morning (Mosley, 2020). Users of caffeine ingest an average of 180 mg per day, the amount of caffeine in two cups of coffee or about one 2-liter bottle of soda (Temple et al., 2017). As is so common, too much of a good thing can be bad for you. The Food and Drug Administration (FDA) has noted that consuming 1,200 mg of caffeine in a day may induce seizures. I know of two individuals with no history of seizures who suddenly had seizures following a large caffeine intake (e.g., two cups of coffee and three energy shots all within about an hour).

When it comes to learning, a moderate amount of caffeine is best. In one study, participants studied images and then ingested 0 mg, 100 mg, 200 mg, or 300 mg of caffeine (Borota et al., 2014). When tested 24 hours later, the participants in the caffeine group did significantly better than the control group, but those who took 200 mg of caffeine did the best. This makes sense as too much caffeine results in many harmful effects such as irritability, anxiety, headaches, rapid heart rate, and extra fatigue when the caffeine wears off.

One concern regarding caffeine is the extent to which it can disrupt your sleep. It does not help to study hard in the evening with a coffee or energy drink if that caffeine keeps you up most of the night. Caffeine has about a 5-hour half-life (Temple et al., 2017). That means if you have an energy drink in the evening to keep you awake while you study, one-half of the potency of that drink will still be in your bloodstream 5 hours later.

Diet

Individuals often don't realize that what they eat will impact their sleep. Sodas and foods with a high fat content (e.g., fast food) have been shown repeatedly to affect sleep. Holmes and colleagues from the University of Massachusetts, Amherst, found that children who consumed fast food tended to sleep less across 24 hours (nighttime sleep and naps; Holmes et al., 2021).

There is also a solid and consistent relationship between weight and sleep deprivation. Studies have shown a relationship between sleep deprivation and obesity in children as young as 4 years old (Miller et al., 2021).

Technology

Technology can seriously interfere with your sleep. If you leave your phone on while you sleep, notifications can make it hard to fall asleep and disrupt your sleep cycles once you are asleep. Setting your phone to "do not disturb" will allow you to sleep without interruption but still allow you to get information if there is an emergency.

The lights on your laptop, phone, and television can also cause difficulty sleeping. Technology typically uses blue-spectrum light, which allows for crisp viewing but also disrupts sleep. Researchers have found that the blue light emitted from phones and laptops interferes with normal melatonin (the hormone that induces sleep) production, tricking your body into a later sleep cycle and making it harder to fall and stay asleep (Snyder & Chang, 2019). The best solution to combat all of this is to simply put electronic devices away before bed. It is also helpful to change the light from blue spectrum to red spectrum by switching to evening mode or downloading an app that will change the light.

Factors That Promote Sleep

There is a lot of good information on the web about good *sleep hygiene*, or the pattern of behaviors that individuals carry out to prepare for sleep. There is variation between people, so you should try different things and go with what works best for you.

If it is within your control, one of the best things you can do is to create an environment that is relaxing and conducive to sleeping, such as a tidy room, curtains that block out light, temperature around 69–71°F, and relative quiet. If you are housing insecure or unable to control your sleeping environment, all you can do is to do the best you can. Any adjustment that helps even a little can have significant benefits.

Bedtime Routine

Adopting a consistent routine provides your mind and body with reassurances and subliminal cues that sleep is natural, welcomed, and anticipated. Initiate a series of quiet activities that allow you to decompress, quiet your thoughts, and relax in your environment. Typical activities include brushing one's teeth, reading a book, stretching, or taking a warm shower. The practice of consistently performing the same activities in the same order develops positive habits that cue your brain that it is time to sleep.

Study Tip 10.3: A good bedtime routine shortens time to fall asleep. Better sleep means better learning.

Physical Activity and Being Outside

Being in nature—sitting near an open window, reading materials under the shade of a tree, walking through dedicated green space, and soaking up some sun—helps promote sleep at bedtime. Interacting with nature supports mental well-being, elevates mood, and fosters a sense of belonging and confidence. Likewise, being in nature routinely leads to measurable reduction in the stress hormone cortisol, lowers reported anxiety, and provides a greater sense of calm. The sun helps to keep circadian rhythms aligned and heavily influences the production of melatonin. Just a bit of sunlight each day has an impact on mood, mental health, and ability to sleep well. Have you noticed that when you spend the day in the sun, you often feel extra tired that evening? That is the power of the sun on setting up melatonin production.

Physical activity is also helpful in promoting efficient sleep with few disruptions. It is best to do more strenuous workouts, particularly intense cardio workouts, in the morning. Some researchers have found that moderate physical activity is more effective for sleep promotion than intense exercise (Wang & Boros, 2019).

Chapter Summary

Researchers have been studying sleep for a very long time. Although we don't know *why* humans sleep, we know sleep is essential. Unfortunately, many college students are sleep deprived, impacting many aspects of life, including course grades. Nearly everyone goes through 90-minute sleep cycles every evening, with REM and deep sleep impacting learning. Our brains are wired to remember information that is deemed necessary. Naps and restful breaks are helpful to get out of sleep debt, provided they are either approximately 20 or 90 minutes in length. Studying all night puts you in a bad learning situation because it is much harder to consolidate memories. Studying all night also immediately puts you into sleep debt, which has additional implications for learning. Several factors can create or add to sleep debt, such as alcohol and caffeine consumption, technology, and ingestion of certain foods before going to bed. Sodas and high-fat foods tend to negatively impact sleep, disrupting the consolidation of information, leading to memory loss of items the day prior. Factors noted in this chapter that promote sleep include the bedroom environment, a bedtime routine, physical activity, being outside, and having a nighttime waking routine. Sleep is something most people do approximately one-third of their lives. Given that time expense, it is worth the energy to manage it the best you can.

Discussion Questions

1 Describe the multiple ways in which a poor night of sleep impacts you the following day.
2 Do you have a time of the day when you are cognitively sharper than other times? How might you (re)schedule some of your responsibilities to take this into account?
3 Do you occasionally have nights where you wake up and have trouble falling back to sleep? If so, what routines do you have, or could you have, to help you get back to sleep? If you do not have difficulty falling back to sleep, what advice would you provide to a friend who is having trouble waking and not being able to fall back to sleep? Note: You cannot use the example from the book.

References

Borota, D., Murray, E., Keceli, G., Chang, A., Watabe, J. M., Ly, M., Toscano, J. P., & Yassa, M. A. (2014). Post-study caffeine administration enhances memory consolidation in humans. *Nature Neuroscience, 17*(2), 201–203. https://doi.org/10.1038/nn.3623

Carskadon, M. A., & Dement, W. C. (2011). Monitoring and staging human sleep. In M. H. Kryger, T. Roth, & W. C. Dement (Eds.), *Principles and practice of sleep medicine* (5th ed.; pp. 16–26). Elsevier Saunders.

Centers for Disease Control and Prevention. (2016, February 18). *1 in 3 adults don't get enough sleep* [Press release]. https://www.cdc.gov/media/releases/2016/p0215-enough-sleep.html

Farhadian, N., Khazaie, H., Nami, M., & Khazaie, S. (2021). The role of daytime naming in declarative memory performance, a systematic review. *Sleep Medicine, 84,* 131–141. https://doi.org/10.1016/j.sleep.2021.05.019

Gais, S., Lucas, B., & Born, J. (2006). Sleep after learning aids memory recall. *Learning and Memory, 13*(3), 259–262. https://doi.org/10.1101/lm.132106

Gilbert, S. P., & Weaver, C. C. (2010). Sleep quality and academic performance in university students: A wake-up call for college psychologists. *Journal of College Student Psychotherapy, 24*(4), 295–306. https://doi.org/10.1080/87568225.2010.509245

Holmes, J., St. Laurent, C. W., & Spencer, R. M. C. (2021). Unhealthy diet is associated with poor sleep in preschool-aged children. *The Journal of Genetic Psychology, 182*(5), 289–303. https://doi.org/10.1080/00221325.2021.1905598

Jarrett, C. (2021, August 14). Early risers and night owls: A neuroscientist explains who is happiest. *Science Focus: The Home of the BBC Science Focus Magazine.* https://www.sciencefocus.com/news/early-risers-and-night-owls-a-neuroscientist-explains-who-is-happiest/

Lemma, S., Berhane, Y., Worku, A., Gelaye, B., & Williams, M. A. (2014). Good quality sleep is associated with better academic performance among university students in Ethiopia. *Sleep and Breathing, 18,* 257–263. https://doi.org/10.1007/s11325-013-0874-8

Mander, B. A., Santhanam, S., Saletin, J. M., & Walker, M. P. (2011). Wake deterioration and sleep restoration of human learning. *Current Biology, 21*(5), 183–184. https://doi.org/10.1016/j.cub.2011.01.019

Martini, M., Martini, C., & Sachse, P. (2019). Brief period of post-encoding wakeful rest support verbal memory retention in children aged 10–13 years. *Current Psychology, 40,* 2341–2348. https://doi.org/10.1007/s12144-019-0156-0

Miller, M. A, Bates, S., Ji, C., & Cappuccio, F. P. (2021). Systematic review and meta-analyses of the relationship between short sleep and incidence of obesity and effectiveness of sleep interventions on weight. *Obesity Reviews, 22*(2), e13113. https://doi.org/10.1111/obr.13113

Mosley, M. (2020, November 21). In praise of caffeine, the world's most widely consumed psychoactive drug. *Science Focus: The Home of BBC Science Focus Magazine.* https://www.sciencefocus.com/the-human-body/in-praise-of-caffeine-the-worlds-most-widely-consumed-psychoactive-drug/

National Center for Health Statistics. (2017). *Health report, United States, 2016: With chartbook on long-term trends in health.* Centers for Disease Control and Prevention. https://www.cdc.gov/nchs/data/hus/hus16.pdf

Okano, K., Kaczmarzyk, J. R., Dave, N., Gabrieli, J. D. E., & Grossman, J. C. (2019). Sleep quality, duration, and consistency are associated with better academic performance in college students. *Science of Learning, 4,* 16. https://doi.org/10.1038/s41539-019-0055-z

Ong, J. L., Te, Y. L., Xuan, K. L., Elaine, v. R., & Chee, M. W. L. (2020). A daytime nap restores hippocampal function and improves declarative learning. *Sleep, 43*(9). http://dx.doi.org/10.1093/sleep/zsaa058

Pietilä, J., Helander, E., Korhonen, I., Myllymäki, T., Kujala, U. M., & Lindholm, H. (2018). Acute effect of alcohol intake on cardiovascular autonomic regulation during the first hours of sleep in a large real-world sample of Finnish employees: Observational study. *JMIR Mental Health, 16*(5), e23. https://doi.org/10.2196/mental.9519

Smith, M. G., Wusk, G. C., Nasrini, J., Baskin, P., Dinges, D. F., Roma, P. G., & Basner, M. (2021). Effects of six weeks of chronic sleep restriction with weekend recovery on cognitive performance and well-being in high-performing adults, *Sleep, 44*(8), 1–14. https://doi.org/10.1093/sleep/zsab051

Snyder, C. K., & Chang, A.-M. (2019). Mobile technology, sleep, and circadian disruption. In M. A. Grander (Ed.), *Sleep and health* (pp. 159–170). Elsevier.

Temple, J., Bernard, C., Lipshultz, S. E., Czachor, D., Westphal, J. A., & Mestre, M. A. (2017). The safety of ingested caffeine: A comprehensive review. *Frontiers in Psychiatry, 8*(80). https://doi.org/10.3389/fpsyt.2017.00080

University of Georgia. (2021, July 12). *Sleep rocks! Health promotion.* https://healthpromotion.uga.edu/sleep/

Wang, F., & Boros, S. (2019). The effect of physical activity on sleep quality: A systematic review. *European Journal of Physiotherapy, 23*(1), 11–18. https://doi.org/10.1080/21679169.2019.1623314

Wilhelm, I., Diekelmann, S., Molzow, I., Ayoub, A., Mölle, M., & Born, J. (2011). Sleep selectively enhances memory expected to be of future relevance. *Journal of Neuroscience, 31*(5), 1563–1569. https://doi.org/10.1523/JNEUROSCI.3575-10.2011

Wong, M. L., Lau, E. Y., Wan, J. H., Cheung, S. F., Hui, C. H., & Mok, D. S. (2013). The interplay between sleep and mood in predicting academic functioning, physical health, and psychological health: A longitudinal study. *Journal of Psychosomatic Research, 74*(4), 271–277. https://doi.org/10.1016/j.jpsychores.2012.08.014

11

EXERCISING TO ENHANCE LEARNING

Research about exercise has come to one overarching conclusion: Exercising is very good for you, and inactivity is very bad for you (Ruegsegger & Booth, 2018). Mark Tarnopolsky, a genetic metabolic neurologist at McMaster University, stated that "if there were a drug that could do for human health everything that exercise can, it would likely be the most valuable pharmaceutical ever developed" (Oaklander, 2016, para. 7). Studies also indicate that regular physical activity makes physiological changes in your body that help you learn faster and remember longer and that students who exercise do better academically (Prina, 2014). This is one of the best ways to learn in harmony with your brain.

General Health Benefits of Physical Activity

Engaging in regular exercise can help maintain a healthy weight; enhance your mood; lower your cholesterol; strengthen bones and improve balance; and lower the risk of some types of cancer, arthritis, and type 2 diabetes (CDC, 2021)! Exercise will also help you sleep better, give you glowing skin, and spark your sex life. Unfortunately, also according to the CDC (2021), only one out of every four adults in the United States reaches the minimum guidelines for aerobic and muscle-strengthening exercises. The good news is that you can adopt a positive lifelong pattern right now. Eighty percent to 85% of adults maintain the physical activity patterns they established as a student in their senior year of college (Sparling, 2003).

The U.S. Department of Health and Human Services (DHHS, 2018) recommends 150 minutes of moderate aerobic activity each week, an average

DOI: 10.4324/9781003499176-15

of about 20 minutes per day. This can be anything that raises your heart rate, including walking, cycling, or water exercises. If you have been living a sedentary life and have not been exercising, you may not be able to immediately engage in an activity that raises your heart rate for 20 minutes. That's okay, you are not alone. A bit more than one-quarter of Americans are inactive (CDC, 2020). Starting or increasing physical activity is important because physical inactivity is a leading risk factor for death worldwide (Huber & Shilton, 2016). The good news is that just 1 hour of moderate-intensity physical activity per week lowers this risk (DHHS, 2018). Just 1 hour per week is an average of about 8 minutes per day! Of course, check with your physician to help you map out a way to get started. Along with aerobic exercise, ask your physician if it is possible for you to engage in strength training for each major muscle groups at least two times per week. Maybe you'll start with 5 or 10 minutes of an exercise that raises your heartrate just a little and work your way up from there. There are many options when it comes to aerobic activity. Anything that raises your heart rate and keeps it in a training zone will work—a very brisk walk; mowing your yard; handcycling, or joining friends for a pickup game of basketball, volleyball, or soccer. For more information about appropriate target heart rates, see the CDC's guide on target heart rates (CDC, 2020).

Not being able to find time to exercise is a primary reason for not being physically active. It can happen to any of us. Fairly recently, I was living a sedentary life. Then I decided I wanted to be part of the 22% of the people exercising and not in the group of 78% lying about feeling sluggish. I know you may be saying you have no time to exercise. There are so many things that just need to be done. That was me as well. Then I did something that helped me get started in a regular physical activity schedule. I set a goal of walking 30 minutes three times a week. To find time to walk, I collected some data. Across 3 days, I wrote down what I spent my time doing each day, all day. I then looked at the list carefully for things I was doing that were more important than living a healthy life, or even living. That made it relatively easy to choose something I could reduce or even stop to carve out the 30 minutes for walking three times a week. Seriously, once you have a list that shows what you are doing, most people can find 30 minutes. If you struggle because you are tired, a 30-minute walk may well energize you. If you can't find 30 minutes, engage in whatever you can, even if it is just 10 minutes.

Basic Brain Structures and Processes

When you engage in activity that raises your heart rate, a host of things happen in your brain that all have the potential to greatly enhance your learning. Of the complex structures and processes going on in your brain at any given moment related to learning, I will mention two that you can directly impact through exercise: the hippocampus and brain-derived neurotrophic factor (BDNF).

Hippocampus

The hippocampus is part of the limbic system, which regulates emotional state and is the organ directly responsible for learning. Its performance can improve or decline over time depending on how much you exercise. The hippocampus coordinates with multiple areas of the brain and is critical in forming long-term memories, consolidating memories, creating long-term potentiation (automaticity), and retrieving memories (Tyng et al., 2017). This is one of the first places in the brain that is damaged by the onset of Alzheimer's disease and other forms of dementia, which is why short-term memory loss is one of the first symptoms noticed in those conditions.

Exercise directly and positively impacts the hippocampus, which directly impacts learning and memory. Brain scans show that when individuals exercise, their hippocampus is very active. Conversely, a sedentary lifestyle negatively impacts the hippocampus and, therefore, makes learning and memory more difficult.

Brain-Derived Neurotrophic Factor

BDNFs are molecules located throughout the brain, primarily in the hippocampus, but also in other organs. They are critical in consolidating memories to be stored for long periods. They provide the tools needed for your brain to collect information, process information, match it to an appropriate schema, and store it in a way that can be recalled later (Miranda et al., 2019). Exercising creates BDNFs, and increased levels of BDNFs translate directly to better learning. It's like fertilizing a plant. Sure, the plant will grow with decent soil and water (not actively generating BDNFs through exercise), but with the proper fertilizer (exercising to increase levels of BDNFs), the plant thrives and blooms. Living a sedentary life can result in reduced levels of BDNFs, which will impair learning (Erickson et al., 2013).

Study Tip 11.1: Aerobic exercise like fast walking, cycling, or running is consistently associated with enhanced learning; just increase your heart rate.

Effects of Long-Term Exercise on Learning

The American Psychological Association (APA) points out many positive aspects of exercise on the human body, including increased blood flow to the brain, which in turn increases thinking and energy levels. Regular exercisers also have better *episodic memory*, the memory system that relates to "episodes" in our lives of people, places, and events. Last but not least, studies show that as people age, active people maintain cognitive functioning more than sedentary people (APA, 2020).

Wendy Suzuki, a professor of neuroscience at New York University, focuses her research on the impact of exercise on mood, learning, memory, and cognition. Suzuki has a TED Talk (see Figure 11.1), *The Brain-Changing Benefits of Exercise*, with about 10 million views where she explains that as she started to exercise, she realized her long-term memory was getting better, her attention was getting better, and her mood was improving. Suzuki notes that when you exercise regularly, you grow new brain cells in areas that help you to learn (TED, 2018).

Study after study finds that physical activity significantly improves the learning process. This is important because individuals who don't know this make poor decisions. For example, primary school programs that take time away from physical education and recess to spend more time studying for state assessment tests typically find that scores decrease. For an extreme example of positive outcomes from a schoolwide physical activity program, see the case study from Naperville, Illinois, in Box 11.1.

Retrieved from https://www.youtube.com/watch?v=BHY0FxzoKZE.

FIGURE 11.1   QR Code for "Wendy Suzuki: The Brain-Changing Benefits of Exercise."

Source: TED (2018).

Box 11.1 Naperville High School Case Study

Administrators at Naperville High School implemented a vigorous program designed to get students physically active. Instead of increasing seat time and having students study more, they realized that fitness and classroom learning were interdependent and believed that exercise would lead to short- and long-term academic benefits. Students took a physical activity class just before their first period (the "zero-hour"), a reading literacy class. The positive effects of the physical exercise program on the reading literacy class were so profound that they renamed the physical education time to "Learning Readiness P.E." Some questioned whether the physical education class immediately before the literacy course was beneficial or whether the exercise program was just beneficial in general. It turns out that some of the students had to take reading literacy later in the day, and students who had reading literacy just after exercise demonstrated about twice the improvement as those with a several-hour gap between exercise and the reading class. The school instituted a Learning Readiness P.E. class just before the afternoon reading literacy course, and the scores in those classes went up as well. By the end of the year, the students in the afternoon literacy course had the same reading level as the morning literacy course. The results were not due to exercise alone, but rather exercise before learning (Robert Wood Johnson Foundation, 2007).

John Ratey (2013), a doctor working at the Harvard Medical School, turned the Naperville experiment into a case study for his book *Spark: The Revolutionary New Science of Exercise and the Brain*. The Naperville students did not just raise their reading scores following the introduction of the zero-hour exercise class. The students also significantly increased their scores on the Trends in International Mathematics and Science Study (TIMSS) test. This is a test for which average U.S. schools struggle to get into the top ten countries. In 1999, eighth graders from Naperville finished first in the world in science and sixth in the world in math (Ratey, 2013). Ratey also noted a 66% decline in behavioral problems, which is consistent with every study involving exercise in that it helps with focus, mood, and attention. For the students at Naperville High School, having a class right after exercise caused all sorts of learning gains.

Effects of Short-Term Exercise on Learning

Although it is ideal to have a long-term exercise program in place, it is really challenging for some individuals to find the time. Luckily, studies have consistently shown increases in attention, working memory, and problem-solving after a single 1-hour exercise session (Chang et al., 2012). In a systematic review of 28 studies investigating the impact of exercise on learning, García-Suárez and colleagues from Mexico, Costa Rica, and Alabama noted that, averaged across studies, a significant amount of BDNF was produced in the hippocampus after just one session of moderate and high-intensity exercise (García-Suárez et al., 2021).

A single workout can improve the ability to shift and focus attention for at least 2 hours (Basso & Suzuki, 2017). In another study, Li and colleagues (2014) at the Ministry of Education in Shanghai, China, studied exercise among college-aged women and found that a single 20-minute workout significantly positively impacted the brain activity associated with working memory.

Timing of Exercise and Learning

When you exercise has an impact on how well you learn. Researchers at Karolinska Institute and Stockholm University found that BDNF levels increased during a cognitive task only when the task was preceded by physical activity (Nilsson et al., 2020). There is value in exercising right before learning. Conversely, there is no—or at least, less—value in exercising right after learning. A team of researchers in the Netherlands tested participants' recall of images if they exercised immediately after or 4 hours after seeing the images (van Dongen et al., 2016). Compared to a control group, there was no increase in recall for those who exercised immediately after seeing the photos, but there was a considerable increase in recall for those who waited 4 hours to exercise.

Study Tip 11.2: Schedule your exercise and most challenging learning together. Exercise and then study within 2 hours to maximize learning.

Therapeutic Exercises

Benefits aren't limited to aerobic exercise. Whether you prefer a less vigorous exercise or are unable to participate in vigorous exercise, *therapeutic exercises* are a great alternative. Therapeutic exercises are those that help the individual focus, use core muscles, develop strength, or quiet the mind. They can include resistance bands, balance ball chairs, pedal exercisers, meditation, walking, yoga, tai chi, and a host of other potential activities. Walking has many positive outcomes, including increasing fitness and enhancing mood, creativity, and cognitive functioning while lowering the risk of heart disease and type 2 diabetes

(DHHS, 2018). Brunner and colleagues at Texas State University, San Marcos, studied the impact of weekly hourlong yoga sessions on cognition (Brunner et al., 2017). University students participated in the sessions for 6 weeks, along with a 10-minute guided meditation each session, and the researchers reported improvement in working memory functioning and attentive mindfulness as a result.

Keep your primary learning goals in mind and identify whether you notice a difference after engaging in these activities. For example, you may find that a stability ball chair helps you focus, or perhaps a meditation session quiets your mind to allow you to process course content more readily. If you may realize a benefit and there are no ill effects, then to me, it seems worth a try.

Chapter Summary

Exercise impacts many aspects of the learning process. These include attention, encoding, consolidation, and automaticity. Although there are many health-related benefits to exercising, nearly three out of four adults in the United States do not engage in regular physical activity. As we have seen, exercise physically impacts the brain, directly affecting learning, as demonstrated by a wide variety of studies looking at the impact of long-term exercise patterns. One-shot exercise programs can also bring about physiological changes in the brain that support learning, memory, or cognition. All exercise is beneficial for learning, but researchers find that exercising directly before a learning episode seems ideal. Therapeutic exercises tend not to have an impact on brain structures, but learners benefit from enhanced mood, creativity, and attention. There are many benefits to being physically active, and the patterns you set now will likely determine the rest of your life. By adhering to exercise, you are changing your life and making learning easier. Consider timing and intensity as possible options for even greater gains. If you are not physically active, there is no better time to start than now. Not only will exercise make it easier for you to learn, it will improve your quality of life.

Discussion Questions

1 If you engage in regular physical exercise, briefly describe the exercise, why you prefer this exercise, and what you see as the primary outcome of exercising regularly. If you do not engage in physical activity regularly, what are your primary reasons for not doing so? Explain what would motivate you to get started and maintain an exercise routine.
2 Watch Dr. Suzuki's TED Talk. Describe the major points you learned from this talk. What information surprised you the most?
3 Why is it important to study one-shot or very brief exercise programs? Explain what you believe is gained by studying these brief exercise findings.

References

American Psychological Association. (2020, March 4). *Working out boosts brain health.* http://www.apa.org/topics/exercise-fitness/stress

Basso, J. C., & Suzuki, W. A. (2017). The effects of acute exercise on mood, cognition, neurophysiology, and neurochemical pathways: A review. *Brain Plasticity, 2*(2), 127–152. https://doi.org/10.3233/BPL-160040

Brunner, D., Abramovitch, A., & Etherton, J. (2017). A yoga program for cognitive enhancement. *PLoS One, 12*(8): e0182366. https://doi.org//10.1371/journal.pone.0182366

Centers for Disease Control and Prevention. (2020). *Target heart rate and estimated maximum heart rate.* https://www.cdc.gov/physicalactivity/basics/measuring/heartrate.htm

Centers for Disease Control and Prevention. (2021). *Benefits of physical activity.* https://www.cdc.gov/physicalactivity/basics/pa-health/index.htm

Chang, Y. K., Labban, J. D., Gapin, J. I., & Etnier, J. L. (2012). The effects of acute exercise on cognitive performance: A meta-analysis. *Brain Research, 1453,* 87–101. https://doi.org/10.1016/j.brainres.2012.02.068

Department of Health and Human Services. (2018). *Physical activity guidelines for Americans* (2nd ed.). U.S. Department of Health and Human Services. https://health.gov/sites/default/files/2019-09/Physical_Activity_Guidelines_2nd_edition.pdf

Erickson, K. I., Gildengers, A. G., & Butters, M. (2013). Physical activity and brain plasticity in late adulthood. *Dialogues in Clinical Neuroscience, 15*(1), 99–108. https://doi.org/10.31887/DCNS.2013.15.1/kerickson

García-Suárez, P. C., Rentería, I., Plaisance, E. P., Moncada-Jiménez, J., & Jiménez-Maldonado, A. (2021). The effects of interval training on peripheral brain derived neurotrophic factor (BDNF) in young adults: A systematic review and meta-analysis. *Science Reports, 11*(1), 8937. https://doi.org/10.1038/s41598-021-88496-x

Huber, L., & Shilton. T. (2016, May 9). *The 4th leading risk factor for death worldwide: physical inactivity is an urgent public health priority.* NCD Alliance. https://ncdalliance.org/news-events/blog/the-4th-leading-cause-of-death-worldwide-physical-inactivity-is-an-urgent-public-health-priority

Li, L., Wei-Wei, M., Yu-Kai, C., Ming-Xia, F., Liu, J., & Gao-Xia, W. (2014). Acute aerobic exercise increases cortical activity during working memory: A functional MRI study in female college students. *PLoS One, 9*(6), e99222. http://dx.doi.org/10.1371/journal.pone.0099222

Miranda, M., Morici, J. F., Zanoni, M. B., & Bekinschtein, P. (2019). Brain-derived neurotrophic factor: A key molecule for memory in the healthy and pathological brain. *Frontiers in Cellular Neuroscience, 13,* 363. https://doi.org/10.3389/fncel.2019.00363

Nilsson, J., Ekblom Ö., Ekblom, M., Lebedev, A., Olga, T., Moberg, M., & Lövdén, M. (2020). Acute increases in brain-derived neurotrophic factor in plasma following physical exercise relates to subsequent learning in older adults. *Scientific Reports, 10,* 4395. http://dx.doi.org/10.1038/s41598-020-60124-0

Oaklander, M. (2016, September 12). The new science of exercise. *Time.* https://time.com/4475628/the-new-science-of-exercise

Prina, L. L. (2014, February 7). Physically fit students do better on academic test scores, says study funded by a Kansas foundation. *Health Affairs Forefront.* https://doi.org.10.1377/forefront.20140207.037053

Ratey, J. (2013). *Spark: The revolutionary new science of exercise and the brain*. Little Brown.

Robert Wood Johnson Foundation. (2007). *Active education: Physical education, physical activity, and academic performance* [Research brief]. https://files.eric.ed.gov/fulltext/ED541165.pdf

Ruegsegger, G. N., & Booth, F. W. (2018). Health benefits of exercise. *Cold Spring Harbor Perspectives in Medicine*, *8*(7), a029694. https://doi.org/10.1101/cshperspect.a029694

Sparling, P. B. (2003). College physical education: An unrecognized agent of change in combating inactivity-related diseases. *Perspectives in Biology and Medicine*, *46*(4), 579–587. https://doi.org/10.1353/pbm.2003.0091

TED. (2018, March 21). *Wendy Suzuki: The brain-changing benefits of exercise* [Video]. *YouTube*. https://www.youtube.com/watch?v=BHY0FxzoKZE

Tyng, C. M., Amin, H. U., Saad, M. N. M., & Malik, A. S. (2017). The influences of emotion on learning and memory. *Frontiers in Psychology*, *8*, 1454. https://doi.org/10.3389/fpsyg.2017.01454

Van Dongen, E. V., Kersten, I. H. P., Wagner, I. C., Morris, R. G. M., & Fernández, G. (2016). Physical exercise performed four hours after learning improves memory retention and increases hippocampal pattern similarity during retrieval. *Current Biology*, *26*, 1722–1727. https://doi.org/10.1016/j.cub.2016.04.071

12

CREATING MORE EFFECTIVE GROUP EXPERIENCES

As an undergraduate I never enjoyed working in groups. Now I realize the problem was not actually with group work, but rather that my classmates and I had never been taught how to work effectively as a group. Researchers from the University of Central Oklahoma and Angelo State University surveyed students and found that although students had an overall negative view of group projects, they saw value in learning to work in groups and indicated that professors should teach students to work well in groups (Ludlum et al., 2021). It is important to note that, done well, working in groups can be pleasant and is undeniably a valuable educational experience, particularly for individuals from marginalized populations. For example, Linda Hodges (2018) at the University of Maryland, Baltimore County, found that although working in structured groups helped all students, it was particularly beneficial for first-generation college students, Black students, economically disadvantaged students, and educationally disadvantaged students.

Along with disciplinary content, college students are often taught broader concepts like the scientific method, how to write research papers, and how to use the library. It would be helpful if instruction specifically on effective group work skills was also regularly taught. Some faculty do teach this skill, but, unfortunately, most do not—probably because they assume that by now you have learned how to work in groups. I hope this chapter provides foundational information to establish or expand on your group work skills.

Benefits of Group Work

Eighty-one percent of job recruiters cite working in a team as a top-of-the-list attribute in job applicants, while less than 60% screen college grads based on

DOI: 10.4324/9781003499176-16

GPA (Koncz & Gray, 2021). There is a reason organizations value individuals who know how to work well in groups. A well-organized team can accomplish amazing outcomes by bringing together individuals with different perspectives.

Develop Soft Skills

Soft skills are essential for thriving professionals. *Hard skills* are the specific behaviors needed to do a job (e.g., bookkeeping, sales, surgical proficiency, computer programming, and analytical skills). *Soft skills* refer to areas such as creativity, adaptability, collaboration, communication, interpersonal communication, and persuasion. Employers now know that although hard skills are needed to get a job done, soft skills are needed to advance an organization. Working effectively in teams is an excellent way to build your soft skills.

Incorporate Diverse Perspectives

When we do a task alone, only one perspective is represented. I have no idea how often I have come up with what I considered to be a brilliant idea, only to have a teammate point out a flaw I missed. Incorporating diverse perspectives is one of my top reasons group projects are so important. As discussed in Chapter 1, diverse perspectives create more substantial outcomes. Admittedly, it has to be a good team that works well together. That is the point of this chapter—how to build good teams and be successful in groups.

Complete Large or Complex Projects

Individuals working well together as a group complete more extensive and complex projects than individuals working independently. Teams create a synergy that generates more ideas than each individual could alone. There are also typical ebbs and flows in an individual's contributions. When a team works together, if one person slows for a bit or gets ill for a few days, the team can continue to make progress. Group cohesiveness is based on coordination, interdependency, and striving for team goals over individual agendas. When those factors are present, it is incredible what a team can accomplish.

Get to Know Group Members

If you will be working together for an extended time, it is helpful to learn some things about one another that can benefit the team. Groups who know and trust each other often become powerful collaborators.

Introductions

At the group's first meeting, take a few minutes for individuals to introduce themselves. This can be relatively fast and could include information that uncovers team members' potential strengths for the project. For the basics, share names, majors, favorite academic areas (may hint at who will be helpful at what), and a hobby. If you are in an asynchronous course, it is beneficial to set up a time to meet virtually to get to know one another. If possible, have your first meeting in person, but a synchronous online meeting is a good alternative for human connection.

Commitment to the Project

This may feel a bit awkward, but it is a cornerstone. Everyone should be honest with the group about what they need or want from this project. Just wanting a C to pass the course is different than wanting an A for graduate school, but both positions may well be appropriate for each of those two students. This is a good discussion to have right away. It can get tricky if you wait until the team is working on the final report.

Competing Demands

It is essential to get a sense of who has competing responsibilities inside and outside of academics. Information about responsibilities such as a small child, a job, or volunteer obligations will help as you schedule meeting times and task due dates. Online meetings may take place in environments with background noise at certain times. Understanding these limitations allows your group to select a time that works best for each student.

Clarify Intended Project Goal

One of the major challenges of working as a group is when members have different ideas as to the direction that should be taken. Take a bit of time at the first group meeting to ensure that everyone in the group has a good sense of what is going to be done. To make sure individuals don't drift off into their own directions, establish foundational goals for the group based on what is in the syllabus:

- How will the work be graded?
- What options are there for the final project (e.g., paper, presentation)?
- When is the project due?
- How must information be submitted (e.g., a presentation only, a presentation and a summary paper)?
- To what extent is it acceptable to ask the faculty member questions or for input during the semester?
- To what extent is it permissible to use generative artificial intelligence (AI) to assist with group work, and how should the use be documented in the final project?
- Can you submit draft material for a cursory read with no grade to ensure the group is going in the right direction?

Once the scope of the project is determined, develop an outline and establish some SMART goals (Chapter 3) to help keep to the plan. The outline can change, but it's important to start with a shared vision. SMART subgoals will minimize misunderstandings. Ambiguous terms like *soon* (when individuals need to have their assignments completed) and *several* (how many references) are defined so they are specific (e.g., next Tuesday and five).

Facilitate Group Processes

If decisions about key aspects of group processes are made at the beginning of the project and followed, the group will be much more effective.

How the Group Will Be Led

After the introductions, confirmation of the task at hand, and the other steps to set the group up to work, the next task is to decide how the group will be led. Different situations call for different structures and arrangements. A leader may be the way to go, or the group members may divide up the activities and get to work without a specific leadership role. The important thing here is to have a conversation to determine what is best for the group.

How Decisions Will Be Made

As you decide how the group will be led, consider how the group will make decisions. The two most common decision-making strategies are voting and consensus. For either approach, agree as soon as possible regarding how decisions will be finalized.

Brainstorm Ideas for Consideration

Brainstorming is a great way to get started on the project. First, review the overall goal or what the faculty member for the course expects from your group. Once you have the problem or goal laid out, next, generate as many ideas as possible in a set amount of time (e.g., 15 minutes). Remember that this is not a competition. There are many different lived experiences, and although some may know more than others at the start, the person who knows the least may have a fresh perspective on the situation. One of the most common errors during brainstorming is to rule out ideas as they are presented or to discuss a presented idea. This is not the time to evaluate ideas. Once the group has listed all the items they can think of, *then* narrow the list of ideas. Discuss which look most promising, which might be modified, and which should be discarded. From here, make an action plan.

Finding the Time to Meet

Scheduling meetings is always a challenge because everyone is busy juggling responsibilities inside and outside academia (e.g., jobs, caretaking, other courses, volunteering). Scheduling meetings well in advance, on a regular basis (e.g., every other Tuesday), and more meetings than you think you'll need are three strategies used by successful leaders. You can always cancel meetings that are not needed, but if you do need time to wrap the project or make last-minute changes, you've already got it blocked off in your members' calendars.

Group Updates and Check-Ins

At each meeting, check on progress and your timeline. It is also valuable for the group leader to check in on group members between meetings to see how work is progressing and whether roadblocks or barriers have arisen. If there is a challenge, it may be possible to immediately bring it up to the group and work toward a solution rather than wait for the next meeting.

Set Ground Rules for the Group

During an initial group meeting, have a brief discussion about past group experiences, what has worked well for each person, and what has not. Life sometimes gets in the way of meetings or completing tasks; do your best to show grace toward that person because we all have issues and challenges we are facing on any given day.

What If Someone Doesn't Do Their Work?

This is a crucial group discussion as it's common for people to fall behind for any number of reasons. Start with a quick conversation with the group member who isn't completing the work and find the root cause of the behavior (O'Hara, 2017). They may have a sick child, their car may not run, they might not understand how to do the work, or they might simply not want to do the work. You won't know unless you talk to the person. Before there is an issue, identify a group policy on handling a situation should a person not complete the work they agreed to do.

What If Someone Misses a Meeting?

There are valid reasons to miss meetings, but members are still responsible for the work they promised to do or are assigned to do. Shared project management trackers or calendars are beneficial in this situation. The person who missed the meeting can send a status report of their work to the group, read notes from the meeting, and do whatever action items were assigned. Being a functional team means joint responsibility and holding each other accountable. Practicing and developing assertive, open communication is as valuable as completing the content of the project.

How to Ensure All Voices Are Heard

Another ground rule for the group may be to affirm that all voices matter and everyone will be heard. Build opportunities for everyone to speak and consider all ideas. Too much of higher education is built for fast-talking, risk-taking, loud extroverts. There is nothing wrong with being any one—or all—of these things. But others should also be given an opportunity to speak and be heard. It is well worth your time to research "reflective and active listening". Listening is an important skill that often needs to be developed. Osten (2016) notes that only about 10% of people listen effectively; most are looking for an opportunity to jump in and offer advice or turn the conversation to themselves.

Addressing Group Conflicts

Some amount of disharmony is almost inevitable when individuals have a shared responsibility to complete a task. That said, if the group openly discusses issues with one another and uses reflective listening, conflicts should be minimal. Expressing differences need not be divisive; there is nothing wrong with disagreements. After all, our goal as educated people is to talk about different perspectives and learn from one another. It can be uncomfortable to have conversation about conflict, but in my experience ignoring a problem nearly always ends up being a bigger problem. If there is a serious conflict, it is best to talk to the course instructor about the situation, particularly if any group member feels unsafe.

Effective Group Meetings

There are many resources in business literature related to running effective meetings. Unfortunately, many people in higher education seem not to know this. When I ask groups of faculty or students to raise their hands if they have been at a poorly run meeting within the past 2 weeks, most hands go up. Running effective meetings need not be elusive. Spend a bit of time learning how to run an effective meeting, and you will be respected by your peers at college and years later at your work. After many years as a faculty member, I am still amazed by individuals who can run effective group meetings.

Agenda

It is an excellent idea to have an agenda and post it ahead of time in your shared meeting notes space. Start the meeting with announcements, but keep them short. Announcements should take no more than a minute or two; a lot can be covered in that time. Next, list the action items with short reports from the members who agreed to complete them. Finally, list what needs to be done next.

Add a line at the bottom of the agenda that says, "Please list here any items you would like to discuss if there is time." If a person has something they want to bring up at the meeting, their concern goes to the bottom of the list, unless the group agrees that their item is critical and time sensitive. This helps keep a meeting productive and minimizes attempts to distract the group.

Study Tip 12.1: Use an agenda for your study group. List what you will do and note times on the agenda to keep the group on track.

Start and End on Time

Start every meeting right on time. People tend to come on time to meetings that start on time. If a person is late, don't revisit items already discussed, or else there is no downside to being late and it slows down group progress. Someone can fill in the late participant very quickly with just the gist of what has been discussed, or the latecomer can refer to shared meeting notes. Also, be efficient and end as quickly as is reasonable. Instead of the traditional hour, try to complete the meeting in 25 minutes—you will probably surprise yourself with the response (Bryant, 2017). I recently had an online meeting with a small group that meets regularly. The entire meeting lasted less than 10 minutes. If meetings are anticipated to be a short check-in, it may be best to meet online.

Assign Group Roles

It's helpful to have roles in place to get the most out of your time and keep track of what was done. Some of the most common roles are:

- *Notetaker*: They record what was discussed and summarize each part of the meeting, any action items, and who will do each item and by when.
- *Monitor*: They keep the group on time and make sure everyone has a chance to speak.

- *Moderator*: If two people are having difficulty understanding each other and seem to be moving toward conflict, the moderator can summarize their statements and explain in different words.
- *Counter-pointer*: Provides a position opposite of what is being seriously considered to avoid groupthink. This is more commonly called "devil's advocate," but who wants to advocate for the devil?
- *Supporter*: This could be a specific role for a group member, or everyone could agree to support one another when ideas are voiced, goals are met, or someone is struggling.

End Meetings With Next Steps

At the end of every meeting, reserve about 5 minutes to review the action items to be done before the next meeting. If someone is working on a large task, break it down so that they can report out on the part that they are to have done at the next meeting. Adam Bryant (2017) suggests that meetings end with a quick summary of who is going to do which tasks and by when will they be done and reported back to the group.

Cancel the Meeting If Possible

Few people like to go to a meeting and have a list of items read to them that could have been emailed. Items on the agenda should be things for which the group needs to come together for synergy and shared knowledge that comes from different lived experiences. It is also a time to support one another. If those things happen, a meeting is a valuable use of time. If synergy and discussions are needed, hold the meeting. If not, then cancel the meeting. Never have a meeting just to see if anyone needs anything.

Study Tip 12.2: Whenever a meeting is cancelled, use that time meaningfully. It is like someone gifted you a bit of time.

Common Group Challenges

After being in countless academic groups and assigning many group projects, the following issues have popped up frequently enough to merit discussion in this book. It is better to be ready rather than be surprised.

Hogs and Logs

There is often someone in the group who wants to take over (a hog)—and just as often someone who doesn't want to do anything (a log). If either of these two personalities arises, it needs to be addressed. This one cannot be left alone because it always gets worse (O'Hara, 2017). One strategy to address this issue is to ask two questions at each meeting: "Do you feel you have been able to contribute as much as you would like? If not, what is an area in which you would like to contribute more or differently?" If someone has not been doing expected work, during check-in the group can say, "Chris, this is the second time you have not done any of the tasks you agreed to do. What is making this challenging for you, and how can we help?" Note that *help* is not just doing the work for Chris, but it is asking how you can be helpful.

Losing the Way

A group may struggle to make progress because they start over multiple times or second-guess their approach. Maybe group members are not meeting deadlines and just stop doing their work. In cases such as these, address the issue and look for a way forward. The worst-case scenario is that the group is stuck and just keeps spinning, not realizing they need a course of action to get out.

Rushing to Wrap

Sometimes a group member just wants the talk to stop and action to start. Moving forward is good; moving too swiftly can cause problems later. Ask the group what needs to be done and how it can be done quickly, but well.

Drama

I have seen more than one group melt down because of drama. By *drama*, I do not mean disagreements because of differing perspectives but rather unprofessional behavior. Unprofessional behaviors are nonproductive and can be harmful. They may include gossiping, blaming, negativity, harassment, undermining, or sabotage. Such behaviors can be addressed when setting the group ground rules. Individuals may not always get along, but they can still work together. If a conflict breaks out during a meeting, summarize the two positions and ask how the disagreement relates to the group task.

Chapter Summary

Group work is an important skill rarely explicitly taught in higher education. Effective groups have several benefits, including developing soft skills, incorporating diverse perspectives, and completing complex projects. As you begin working on the project, clarify the assignment so everyone understands the identified successful outcome.

Once a decision has been made regarding how best to work together, outline expectations of group members, and determine consequences for breaking group policies. To ensure an effective meeting, set an agenda, start and end on time, assign roles to group members, check in on the well-being of members, and cancel the meeting if it is not needed. Finally, note that common group challenges require attention, or they will get worse. It is important to balance the final output of the assigned group work with the development of professional behaviors within the group.

Discussion Questions

1 What has been your overall experience working in groups? Think of a time when a group you were in worked well and a time when a group did not work well. List factors that have been present in good and bad experiences. What would you change?
2 Why do you think students are rarely taught how to work well in groups? Do you feel that teaching students to be effective group members should be part of any class that assigns groups? If so, what are a few things that should be taught to undergraduates about working in groups?
3 Explain three ground rules you feel are essential for any group. Explain with enough detail that someone reading them would understand your position only from what is written. You may identify three from this chapter or another source.

References

Bryant, A. (2017, April 24). How to run a more effective meeting. *New York Times: Business*. https://www.nytimes.com/guides/business/how-to-run-an-effective-meeting

Hodges, L. C. (2018). Contemporary issues in group learning in undergraduate science classrooms: A perspective from student engagement. *CBE-Life Sciences Education, 17*(2), 1–10. https://doi.org/10.1187/cbe.17-11-0239

Koncz, A., & Gray, K. (2021, April 13). *The key attributes employers seek on college graduates' resumes*. National Association of Colleges and Employers. https://www.naceweb.org/about-us/press/the-key-attributes-employers-seek-on-college-graduates-resumes/

Ludlum, M., Conklin, M., & Tiger, A. (2021). Group projects in higher education: How demographic factors affect student perceptions of grading, leadership roles, assessment, and applicability. *Journal of Higher Education Theory and Practice, 21*(1), 13–27. http://dx.doi.org/10.2139/ssrn.3757526

O'Hara, C. (2017). *How to work with someone who isn't a team player*. Harvard Business Review Online. https://hbr.org/2017/04/how-to-work-with-someone-who-isnt-a-team-player

Osten, C. (2016, October 5). *Are you really listening, or just waiting to talk?* Psychology Today. https://www.psychologytoday.com/us/blog/the-right-balance/201610/are-you-really-listening-or-just-waiting-talk

A MESSAGE FROM DR. Z

Welcome to the end of this book! If it is the end of the semester for you, I hope that things went well and that the experiences you had over the past few months brought added richness to your perspective. If you received this book as a high school graduation gift and are heading off to college soon, I hope you spend your first semester building a better understanding of the individuals you are fortunate enough to meet.

Now for the rest of my story. In the introduction of this book, I noted that if Dr. Sawyer had signed my drop slip, I would have dropped out of Lake Superior State College and returned to my small hometown of Cadillac, Michigan. I would have gotten a job there and made a life. However, Dr. Sawyer didn't sign the paper, so I continued my studies. My family didn't have the means to provide financial support, so I worked, a lot. I understand what it is to work to exhaustion and then some to pay for college. It is so hard. If that is you, keep your head up and keep moving ever forward.

I got married just before the start of my junior year. We found strength in each other that got us through many rough times. My wife was also a first-generation college student who ended up with a master's degree in nursing. Because of my rough first year of college, I needed extra time to graduate. If it takes you an additional year or two or three to graduate, persevere and keep moving forward.

I completed my psychology degree and because I was the student government president, I ended up being the student speaker at graduation. There I was, on a stage in front of thousands of people, when just a few years prior, I was terrified to give a presentation in a speech class of 15 students. Fear will give way if you push at it long enough, with gentle pressure relentlessly applied. Stay brave and always move forward.

I went to graduate school at Ohio University. As an undergraduate, I didn't have great grades, but I had relevant experiences and a passion for what I wanted to pursue. In the process of applying for a graduate program in Industrial/Organizational Psychology I received rejections from seven universities. If your grades are not great, don't give up. There will come a day when the degree is essential, but the grades are irrelevant. Do the best you can and keep moving forward.

My wife and I had our first child while I was in graduate school, so I understand balancing academic, financial, and family demands. It was challenging to find a full-time teaching job following graduate school, but I knew what I wanted to do. You may have trouble finding balance while also finding your first professional job; hang in there and keep pushing forward.

I finally got a teaching job at Southern Oregon State College, seven years later I moved to Central Michigan University, then seven years later I moved to the University of North Carolina at Chapel Hill. After all of that, I landed in the UNC School of Medicine, and have been at UNC for more than 15 years. In 2019 I returned to Lake Superior State University as the commencement speaker, where I received an honorary doctorate. On that stage, looking at the same size audience that I had stood before many years prior, the audience seemed smaller, because my world had gotten larger. I told the graduates and their parents about my F minus minus, the withdrawal slip almost signed, and that I am now a first-generation college student teaching teachers how to teach at a school I could never have gotten into as a student. In the graduation speech, I talked about possibilities, drive, and, of course, always moving forward.

You will not have the same battles I did, but you will have battles. Fight through your challenges and always take time to celebrate your wins. You will have many victories. I wish I had taken more time to celebrate each victory. I can say without reservation that the world needs the person you can become. You are a steward of our future. I wrote Chapter 1 about perspectives, acceptance, and enriching who you are because I believe that above all else. Surround yourself with bright, positive, and accepting individuals who are different from you, so that you will grow from their perspectives. Do that and you will achieve great things. Regardless of how busy you are, take time to explore as you move forward.

I leave you with the following to consider in the months ahead. Be mindful of your past but look to the future. Listen carefully to the voices of others and find respectful ways for your voice to be heard. Get credit for your accomplishments without taking anything away from others. Most importantly, always strive for more so that you have more you can share. Ever forward.

If you find this book of value, or if you see something in need of correction, please send me an email: toddzakrajsek@gmail.com.

Respectfully,
Dr. Z

ABOUT THE AUTHOR

Todd D. Zakrajsek, PhD, is an associate professor in the Department of Family Medicine at The University of North Carolina at Chapel Hill and president of the International Teaching Learning Cooperative (ITLC). He currently directs four ITLC-Lilly Conferences on Evidence-Based Teaching and Learning. Todd was a tenured associate professor of psychology and built faculty development efforts at three universities before joining the UNC School of Medicine. At UNC, he provides resources for faculty on various topics related to teaching/learning, leadership, and scholarly activity. Todd has served on many educationally related boards and work groups, including *The Journal of Excellence in College Teaching, International Journal for the Scholarship of Teaching and Learning, College Teaching,* and *Education in the Health Professions.* He has consulted for and worked with organizations such as the American Council on Education (ACE), Lenovo Computer, Microsoft, and the Bill and Melinda Gates Foundation. He has delivered keynote addresses and campus workshops at hundreds of conferences and university campuses in 49 states, 12 countries, and 4 continents. Todd's recently co-authored books include *Dynamic Lecturing* (2017); *Teaching for Learning, Second Edition* (2021); *Advancing Online Teaching* (2021); *The New Science of Learning, Third Edition* (2022); *Teaching at Its Best, Fifth Edition* (2023); and *Classroom Assessment Technique, Third Edition* (2024). More details about Todd's work are located at https://www.toddzakrajsek.com.

INDEX

Printed in the United States
by Baker & Taylor Publisher Services